# Agency and Necessity

## Great Debates in Philosophy

*Personal Identity*
Sydney Shoemaker and Richard Swinburne

*Consciousness and Causality*
D. M. Armstrong and Norman Malcolm

*Agency and Necessity*
Antony Flew and Godfrey Vesey

# Agency and Necessity

*Antony Flew*
*and Godfrey Vesey*

Basil Blackwell

First published 1987

Basil Blackwell Ltd
108 Cowley Road, Oxford, OX4 1JF, UK

Basil Blackwell Inc.
432 Park Avenue South, Suite 1503
New York, NY 10016, USA

*British Library Cataloguing in Publication Data*

Flew, Antony
  Agency and necessity.—(Great debates in
  philosophy)
  1. Causation
  I. Title.  II. Vesey, Godfrey  III. Series
  122    BD591

  ISBN 0–631–14539–7
  ISBN 0–631–14541–9 Pbk

*Library of Congress Cataloging in Publication Data*

  Flew, Antony, 1923–
  Agency and necessity.
  (Great debates in philosophy)
  Bibliography: p. 175
  Includes indexes.
  1. Agent (Philosophy)  2. Necessity (Philosophy)
3. Causation.  I. Vesey, Godfrey Norman Agmondisham, 1923–
II. Title.  III. Series.
BD450.F548  1987  123  86–30957
ISBN 0–631–14539–7
ISBN 0–631–14541–9 (pbk.)

Typeset in 11 on 13 pt Sabon
by Cambrian Typesetters, Frimley, Surrey
Printed in Great Britain by Billing & Sons Ltd, Worcester

# Contents

# Great Debates in Philosophy

Since the time of Socrates, dialogue has been a powerful means of philosophical exploration and exposition. By presenting important current issues in philosophy in the form of a debate, this series attempts to capture the flavour of philosophical argument and to convey the excitement generated by the interplay of ideas.

There will normally be more than two sides to any argument, and for any two 'opponents' there will be points of agreement as well as points of disagreement. The debate will not, therefore, necessarily cover every aspect of the chosen topic, nor will it present artificially polarized arguments. The aim is to provide, in a thought-provoking format, a series of clear, accessible and concise introductions to a variety of subjects, ranging from formal logic to contemporary ethical issues. The series will be of interest to scholars, students and general readers alike, since each book brings together two outstanding philosophers to throw light on a topic of current controversy.

The first essay states a particular position and the second essay responds to it. The dialogue then continues through further exchanges between the authors. If the resulting book gives rise in its turn to further discussion, argument and debate among its readers, it will have achieved its purpose.

# Plato's Two Kinds of Causes

GODFREY VESEY

# 1  B. F. Skinner on the Control of Human Behaviour

Some of the great debates in philosophy are on meta-physical issues that are far removed from everyday concerns. These issues are debated only by professional philosophers, not by psychologists, sociologists or social workers. Conclusions of these debates would have no bearing on how we should manage our lives, or deal with our fellow human beings. In short, such issues are academic, in the modern sense of 'academic'.

This is not the case with the issue to be debated in this volume. The issue is that of agency and necessity: human agency and causal necessity. It is fundamental to questions of how we should manage our lives and treat one another. According to one possible conclusion of the debate it is an illusion that we manage our lives at all, an illusion born of ignorance of the way we are caused to behave as we do.

This being the sort of issue under debate, it is not surprising to find non-philosophers writing on the subject. One is the behaviourist psychologist B. F. Skinner (1904– ). In his book *Beyond Freedom and Dignity*, first published in 1971, he writes:

> In what we may call the pre-scientific view . . . a person's behaviour is at least to some extent his own achievement. He is free to deliberate, decide, and act, possibly in original ways, and he is to be given credit for his successes and blamed for his failures. In the scientific view . . . a person's behaviour is determined by a genetic endowment traceable to the evolutionary history of the species and by the environmental circumstances to which as an individual he has been exposed. Neither view can be proved, but it is in the nature of scientific inquiry that the evidence should shift in favour of the second. As we learn more about the effects of the environment, we have less reason to attribute any part of human behaviour to an autonomous controlling agent (Skinner, 1973, p. 101).

Skinner ascribes 'the pre-scientific view' of human behaviour to the early Greeks, especially Plato and Aristotle. He says that whereas Greek physics and biology led eventually to modern science, Greek theories of human behaviour led nowhere. 'Their way of thinking about human behaviour must have had some fatal flaw', he says (ibid., p. 12). The flaw was that of attributing behaviour to an 'indwelling agent' (ibid., p. 13), who behaves as he does because of 'intentions, purposes, aims, and goals' (ibid., p. 14). It is a flaw that has persisted even into the thinking of intelligent people today. We attribute behaviour to an 'inner man'. Skinner writes:

> The function of the inner man is to provide an explanation which will not be explained in turn. Explanation stops with him. He is not a mediator between past history and current behaviour, he is a *centre* from which behaviour emanates. He initiates, originates, and creates, and in doing so he remains, as he was for the Greeks, divine. We say that he is autonomous – and, so far as a science of behaviour is concerned, that means miraculous (ibid., p. 19).

Skinner makes no secret of his own purpose in discrediting the notion that human behaviour is to be attributed to 'autonomous agents'. It is to gain acceptance for the notion that psychologists should apply what they know, of the way people's behaviour is determined by their environment, to *controlling* how other people behave.

He refers, in this connection, to the work of the British reformer and socialist Robert Owen (1771–1858). In 1816 Owen published a book the title of which was *A New View of Society, or Essays on the Formation of the Human Character, Preparatory to the Development of a Plan for gradually ameliorating the Condition of Mankind*. Skinner approves of Owen's aim – the aim of ameliorating the condition of mankind – but says that little could be expected to come of Owen's plan because Owen and others at the time did not know enough about how human behaviour is determined by the environment. 'We must know how the environment works', Skinner says, 'before we can change it to change behaviour. A mere shift in emphasis from man to environment means very little' (ibid., p. 181).

It is, Skinner holds, the new behaviourist psychology, to which he has himself contributed, that will make possible the fulfilment of plans for ameliorating the condition of mankind. The old introspectionist associationist psychology is no good for this.

Skinner writes:

> Some philosophers have tried to stay within the world of the mind, arguing that only immediate experience is real, and experimental psychology began as an attempt to discover the mental laws which governed interactions among mental elements . . . The world of the mind steals the show. Behaviour is not recognized as a subject in its own right (ibid., p. 17).

Only when behaviour is recognized as a subject in its own right, and the laws that govern the way in which a person's behaviour is determined by his environment are known, will it be possible to fulfill plans like those of Robert Owen.

> An experimental analysis shifts the determination of behaviour from autonomous man to the environment – an environment responsible both for the evolution of the species and for the repertoire acquired by each member . . . A scientific view of man offers exciting possibilities. We have not yet seen what man can make of man (ibid., p. 210).

Owen, in his day, was accused by John Stuart Mill of having 'most perversely misunderstood' the doctrine 'that our characters follow from our organisation, our education, and our circumstances' (Mill, [1843] 1974, VI.ii.3). Owen had thought the doctrine meant a person cannot form his own character (Owen, [1816] 1972, p. 91). Mill rejects this conclusion: 'We are exactly as capable of making our own character, *if we will*, as others are of making it for us' (Mill, [1843] 1974, VI.ii.3).

In our day, Skinner has been accused of the faults of the behaviourist school of psychology that dominated American psychology from the 1930s to the 1960s:

> The apparent extreme environmentalism of this school, which developed around Watson and later B. F. Skinner, serves merely to hide its impoverished concept of humanity and its manipulative approach to the control of human beings, evidenced by Skinner's concern with the control and manipulation of behaviour, in children or prisoners, by a superior cadre of value-free demigods in white coats, who are to decide on the correct behaviour into which they will coerce their victims (Rose et al., 1984, p. 78).

If Skinner has an 'impoverished concept of humanity', in what does the impoverishment consist? The Greeks, if he is right about their attributing human behaviour to an 'indwelling agent', might say that his concept of humanity is impoverished precisely because he rejects the notion of agency. Is Skinner right about the Greeks? And is he right about the notion of agency being one we can well do without, a 'fatal flaw' in our thinking?

## 2 Agent Causation and Event Causation

Although Plato does not write about 'agency and necessity', he does write about 'necessity'. In his account of the making of the world (*Timaeus* 46c–48a; cf. *Laws* X 894d–898c) he says the world is 'the combined work of necessity and mind'. What lies behind this remark is a distinction between two different kinds of causes. On the one hand, there are things 'which are endowed with mind and are the workers of things fair and good'. On the other, there are things like fire and water, earth and air, 'things which, being moved by others, are compelled to move others'. Plato says that the kinds of causes that, being moved by others, are compelled to move others, cooperate with, but are secondary to, causes of the other kind, the ones that have mind and work things fair and good. Most people, he says, think that things like fire and water, earth and air are 'the prime causes of all things, because they freeze and heat, and contract and dilate, and the like', but they are not, 'for they are incapable of reason or intellect'.

In Plato's remark, in the *Timaeus*, that the world is the combined work of necessity and mind, the 'mind' is not a human mind. It is the mind of a craftsmanlike God. This being so, it is not obvious what relevance, if any, his distinction between two kinds of causes, and his remark about causes of one kind cooperating with, but being secondary to, causes of the other kind, has to the question of human agency and necessity. To see any relevance one needs to see what the doctrine about two kinds of causes, and their relationship, amounts to in the case of human beings. Obligingly, Plato tells us – in the *Phaedo* 98c–99b).

Socrates has been condemned to die, by drinking hemlock, for 'not believing in the gods the state believes in, and introducing different new divine powers; and also for corrupting the young'. He can either await the arrival of the poison-bearer, or he can take to his heels and run away. He sits down, to await the poison-bearer. The question is: what is the cause of his sitting down?

Socrates, in the dialogue, compares two different answers:

(a) The reason why I am lying here now is that my body is composed of bones and sinews, and since the bones move freely in their joints the sinews by relaxing and contracting enable me somehow to bend my limbs, and that is the cause of my sitting here in a bent position.

(b) Since Athens has thought it better to condemn me, therefore I for my part have thought it better to sit here, and more right to stay and submit to whatever penalty she orders. Because, by dog, I fancy that these bones and sinews would have been in the neighbourhood of Megara or Boeotia long ago if I did not think it was more right and honourable to submit to whatever penalty my country orders than to take to my heels and run away.

Socrates says that the answer of the second kind, (b), provides the *real* reason for his sitting or lying down:

If it were said that without bones and sinews I should not be able to do what I think is right, it would be true. But to say that it is because of them that I do what I am doing, and not through choice of what is best, would be a very lax and inaccurate form of expression. Fancy being unable to distinguish between the cause of a thing and the condition without which it could not be a cause.

The kind of answer of which (a) is an example is an answer in terms of the kind of cause that Plato says is governed by necessity. If Socrates' sinews contract, then, provided his bones are rigid and move freely in their joints, his legs *must* bend, with the result that he assumes a sitting or lying position. Necessity governs his bodily parts. The kind of answer of which (b) is an example is in terms of the kind of cause Plato says has mind. Socrates, the human being, has a mind. He does what he does 'through choice of what is best'.

So much for Plato's distinction between two kinds of causes, as it applies to human actions. Now, what is meant by saying, in the case of human actions, that the causes that are governed by necessity cooperate with, but are secondary to, those that have mind?

What Socrates says about the real reason for his sitting down provides the answer. By the causes that are governed by necessity being secondary to those that have mind, he means that what *his legs* do (movements for sitting or movements for running) depends on what *he* does (decides to stay), rather than it being the case that what *he* does (decides to stay) depends on what *his legs* do. By the causes that are governed by necessity cooperating with those that have mind, he means that if he decides to stay then his legs move appropriately (movements for sitting, rather than for running). As a rule the causes that govern by necessity do cooperate with those that have mind, but there are exceptions, the most extreme being when someone is totally paralysed.

Plato's distinction between two kinds of causes, those 'which are endowed with mind and are the workers of things fair and good' and those 'which, being moved by others, are compelled to move others', is represented, in recent philosophy, by a distinction between 'agent causation' and 'event causation'.

The terms 'agent causation' and 'event causation', or very similar expressions, were first used in the 1960s (Chisholm, 1964; Taylor, 1966; Yolton, 1966; Kolnai, 1966; Thalberg, 1967; Davidson, 1968). Although the philosophers who use them do not acknowledge any debt to Plato, the distinction they make between agent causation and event causation would appear to be the same as Plato's between the causes that have mind and those that govern by necessity. Plato's example can be used to illustrate the modern philosophers' distinction just as well as it illustrates his own. Socrates sitting down because he thinks it better to do what he thinks is right is an example of agent causation. His muscles relaxing or contracting causing his bones to move in their joints so that his legs bend or straighten is an example of event causation.

What are the main characteristics of the two kinds of causation? Plato draws our attention to two characteristics of event causation when he says that fire and water, earth and air are 'things which, being moved by others, are compelled to move others'. First, the causing event is itself caused, and, if it is caused by another event, that event, too, is caused — and so on, and so on. Event causation is inherently chain-like, the chain being endless. Secondly, in a causal chain one event does not simply follow on another event, and precede a further event; there is an element of compulsion about the succession. There is some sort of necessary connection between a causing event and its effect.

A third characteristic is that the same causing event always causes the same effect. Event causation is essentially law-governed.

Fourthly, how do we find out what causes what, in event causation? It is not simply by registering what is perceived to follow what. If it were, then since day, in Spain, is perceived always to follow night, we would conclude that night, in Spain, causes day. We make hypotheses as to what the cause of some event is, and then test the hypotheses experimentally. In this way we come to conclusions which go beyond what can be directly experienced. We cannot perceive the earth stopping revolving on its axis (because it does not stop doing so), but we can come to the conclusion, as a result of our experiments, that *if* the earth were to stop revolving on its axis then night, in Spain, would not be followed by day. It is of the essence of event causation that it covers what would happen *if*.

Finally, there is the point on which Hume insists. 'The mind can never find the effect in the supposed cause, by the most accurate scrutiny and examination. For the effect is totally different from the cause, and consequently can never be discovered in it.' Even after finding out what the effect of a given event is 'there are always many other effects, which, to reason, must seem fully as consistent and natural' (Hume, [1748] 1975, para. 25). In other words, cause and effect are not *internally* related: one can describe the cause independently of the effect. Hume insists on this being a feature of event causation because he is an empiricist; as such, he is bound to hold that the effect of a given event can be found out only by observation and experience.

In contrast with event causation, agent causation is characterized by agents *not* being moved by others, and hence *not* compelled to move others. Agents are beginners of motion, and are at liberty to move or not. Being at liberty, they are morally responsible for what they do. Agent causation is not law-governed. It is characterized by the agent's being mindful of what he is doing in a way in which things without minds cannot be. 'Being mindful' means that an agent can say what he is doing, in the sense of what he is up to, without having to observe his behaviour; and that if he is doing it with some end in view he can say what that end is.

Finally, agent causation is characterized, for its effectiveness in bodily movements, by its dependence on event causation. Socrates can sit down only because certain bodily events do cause other bodily events; when certain of his muscles contract, certain bones moves in their joints, so that his legs bend. If his muscles were atrophied, or his bones made incapable of moving in their joints by arthritis, he would not be able to move his limbs.

The feature of event causation philosophers find most attractive is that it is essentially law-governed. Thus Donald Davidson writes:

> We explain a broken window by saying that a brick broke it; what explanatory power the remark has derives from the fact that we may first expand the account of the cause

to embrace an event, the movement of the brick, and we can then summon up evidence for the existence of a law connecting such events as motions of medium-sized rigid objects and the breaking of windows. The ordinary notion of cause is inseparable from this elementary form of explanation. But the concept of agent-causation lacks these features entirely. What distinguishes agent-causation from ordinary causation is that no expansion into a tale of two events is possible, and no law lurks. By the same token, nothing is explained (Davidson, 1980, p. 53).

The most attractive feature of agent causation is that it involves a beginning of motion. In event causation we observe only a transference, not a production, of motion. This is why John Locke (1632–1704) who does not recognize agent causation and event causation as two distinct kinds of causation, nevertheless says that the mind receives 'its *idea* of *active power* clearer from reflection on its own operations than it doth from any external sensation' (Locke, [1690] 1975, II.xxi.4).

The most problematic feature of event causation, especially for empiricists, concerns the necessity with which an effect follows its cause. How do we get this idea of a necessary connection? We shall consider Hume's treatment of this question in due course.

The most problematic feature of agent causation is its dependence on event causation. What form does the dependence take? Plato makes Socrates say: 'The sinews by relaxing and contracting enable me somehow to bend my limbs'. The word 'somehow' invites the question 'how?'. Does Socrates use his sinews to move his limbs as he might use a stick to move a stone? Plato does not commit himself, but the question is taken up by Aristotle, in his *Physics*.

# 3 Basic Actions: Aristotle and Descartes

At the beginning of Book 8, Chapter 5, of his *Physics*, Aristotle considers the case of a man moving a stone with a stick held in his hand. Whereas the man moves the stone by doing something else (namely, hitting it with the stick), and moves the stick by doing something else (namely, moving the hand in which he is holding it), he does *not*, Aristotle implies, move his hand by doing something else. He moves it *immediately*. In other words, his muscles are not instruments he uses to make his hands move. He cannot move his hand immediately *unless* his muscles can contract and relax, but he does not make his hand move *by* contracting and relaxing his muscles. This is how Aristotle answers the question of the nature of the dependence of agent causation on event causation.

Aristotle's notion of immediate movement is represented, in recent philosophy, by the notion of 'basic action', a term that was first used, like 'agent causation' and 'event causation', in the 1960s (Danto, 1963). Expressed in this modern terminology, Aristotle's position is that the man's movement of his hand is a basic action. There is no other action the man performs that causes his hand to move, as moving his hand causes the stick held in it to move.

The significance of Aristotle's view that a man can move his hand immediately, even though he can do so only because his bones can move in their joints, his muscles contract and relax, and so on, can be brought out by considering a case mentioned by William James in his *Principles of Psychology* (James, 1891, vol. II, p. 105). A patient has anaesthesia of the moving parts. If he raises his hand he cannot feel it rising. If someone holds it, he cannot feel it being held. He is willing to do whatever he is told to do. The experimenter closes the patient's eyes, holds his anaesthetic arm still, and tells the patient to raise his hand to his head. When the patient opens his eyes, James says, 'he will be astonished to find that the movement has not taken place'. Evidently the patient thought he had done as he was told; he thought he had raised his hand. He thought this until he opened his eyes and found the movement had not taken place.

Suppose, now, that the question is asked, 'Did the patient do anything to make him think he had raised his hand?' The significance of Aristotle's view about basic actions is that his uncompromising answer to this question is: 'No. It seemed to him as if he raised his hand (apart from his not feeling it rise), but in fact he did not do anything.' Many people would not find this answer acceptable. They would want to be able to say that the patient had some reason for thinking he had raised his hand other than simply that it seemed to him that he had raised it. He must have *done* something, they would say, otherwise why should it even seem to him that he had raised it?

People who cannot accept Aristotle's answer are likely to opt for one of three other answers. Of the three, the least popular is that the patient did whatever muscle contractions, and so on, would ordinarily have made his arm rise. This is not a popular answer because of the inclination to adopt the principle that a person cannot be said to do something he is not conscious of, unless it is an unintended effect of something else he does. On this principle, muscle contractions are no more actions than are the impulses down the nerves from the brain to the muscles.

A more popular answer is that the patient *tried* to raise his hand. I considered this answer in a paper I wrote about twenty-five years ago, and dismissed it as follows:

But this is unsatisfactory in that the patient may be unaware of any difficulty in moving his hand. Because of his anaesthesia it is not as if he could feel his hand being held down. From the patient's point of view it is not as if he had to try to move his hand, but as if he could actually, and easily, move it – or, at least, it is like this until he opens his eyes.

In short, 'He tried to move his hand' describes not so much what the patient did as what he did not do: he failed to qualify for the description 'He moved his hand' (Vesey, 1961, p. 353).

I was not, at the time, concerned to relate the 'trying' answer to the Aristotelian answer. How does it relate? Or, rather, how do the advocates of the 'trying' answer (O'Shaughnessy, 1973; McCann, 1975; Hornsby, 1980, ch. 3) intend it to relate? Do they think of trying as a basic action, and hence hold Aristotle to have been mistaken in holding that the stone-mover, in his example, moves his hand immediately? To make the stone move, Aristotle says, the man does something else: he hits it with the stick. Do the advocates of the 'trying' answer hold that to make his hand move a man does *something else* (that is, *tries* to make it move)? Is trying to do A an act that can be described independently of A? Or is trying internally related to doing? (According to Hume, if it is internally related then the trying/doing relationship does not qualify to be an instance of event causation.)

The answer is that some advocates of the 'trying' answer seem to think it commits them to denying that moving a limb is a basic action, while others seem to think that the relationship of trying to doing is internal. Thus, McCann writes:

Recent philosophers . . . have viewed one's moving a limb as normally a basic or simple action, whose performance involves no instrumental means. But this seems to conflict with empirical evidence. Even a cursory look at the medical literature on testing for deficiencies in the power of movement indicates that a paralytic *can* try to make what appear to be normal movements (McCann, 1975, p. 428).

On the other hand, O'Shaughnessy says that the ultimate

16 *Godfrey Vesey*

psychological description of someone's trying to raise his arm is: trying to raise the arm (O'Shaughnessy, 1973, pp. 373, 375, 378, 386), that the act of trying is not independently specifiable (p. 377) and that the trying and the arm rising are 'made for each other' (pp. 383, 385, 386). He evidently holds that the trying and the arm rising *are* distinct in the sense that the trying could occur without the arm rising (ibid., p. 373), but are *not* distinct in the sense that, in Humian terminology, 'the effect is totally different from the cause, and consequently can never be discovered in it'. O'Shaughnessy says that the trying/raising relationship is causal, but he would not say, about the effect of trying to raise an arm, that 'there are always many other effects, which, to reason, must seem fully as consistent and natural' (Hume). The causal power of trying, he says, 'cannot be an external property like the power of a thought to cause goose pimples' (ibid., p. 379).

We have been considering possible answers to the question 'Did the patient do anything to make him think he had raised his hand?' I said that Aristotle's own answer would be 'No. It seemed to him as if he raised his hand, but in fact he did not do anything', and that many people would not find this answer acceptable. They would opt for one of three alternative, affirmative, answers. We have considered two of them; the third is the answer that would have been given by René Descartes (1596–1650), had the question been put to him: the patient *willed* his hand to rise, he performed an 'operation of will'.

Descartes gives this answer in the 'Arguments' appended to his reply to the second set of objections to the *Meditations* (1641). He writes:

> *Thought.* I use this term to include everything that is within us in such a way that we are immediately aware of it. Thus all the operations of the will, the intellect, the imagination and the senses are thoughts. I say 'immediately' so as to exclude the consequences of thoughts; a voluntary movement, for example, originates in a thought but is not itself a thought.

*Idea.* I understand this term to mean the form of any given thought, immediate perception of which makes me aware of the thought. (Descartes, [1641] 1985, vol. II, p. 113).

There are four points to note about this answer. First, it involves a concept of *willing* that the Greeks would not have recognized. To 'will', in Greek thought, is not to exercise an independent mental faculty called 'the will'; it is to adopt a favourable attitude to some specific object (Pohlenz, 1959, I, p. 124; Long, 1971, p. 192). For Descartes, on the other hand, there are 'operations of the will' on a par with those of the intellect, the imagination and the senses. Descartes may even have introduced this concept of the will, and willing.

Secondly, when a new concept is introduced there are always questions about how it relates to existing concepts. Descartes says that voluntary movements are 'consequences' of operations of the will. Does he mean *causal* consequences? And if he does mean causal consequences, what does he mean by 'causal'? Does he mean by a causal relationship the sort of external relationship Hume means: a relationship such that 'the effect is totally different from the cause, and consequently can never be discovered in it' and such that even after finding out what the effect of a given event is 'there are always many other effects, which, to reason, must seem fully as consistent and natural'?

Thirdly, Descartes evidently thinks of thoughts as having a perceptible or phenomenal character. An 'idea' is a thought *qua* perceptible. In this he was followed by John Locke, who called a person's perception of the operations of his mind 'reflection', and said that 'though it be not sense, as having nothing to do with external objects, yet it is very like it, and might properly enough be called internal sense' (Locke, [1690] 1975, II.i.4).

Fourthly, Descartes' answer, including the notion that thoughts have a phenomenal or perceptible character, became the established orthodoxy. Everyone started talking about mental or psychological *phenomena*, much as they talked about physical or physiological phenomena. What Locke had called 'reflection' William James called 'introspection', a word, he said, that 'need hardly be defined – it means, of course, the looking into our own minds and reporting what we there discover' (James, 1891, vol. 1, p. 185). James, like Descartes, called the thought *qua* inwardly perceived an 'idea'. He said that 'volition is a psychic or moral fact pure and simple', and that the bodily movements which ensue 'are exclusively physiological phenomena, following according to physiological laws upon the neural events to which the idea corresponds' (ibid., vol. II. p. 560).

This leaves us with the two questions: When Descartes says that voluntary movements are consequences of operations of the will, does he mean causal consequences? And, if he does, does he mean by a causal relationship the sort of external relationship Hume means?

One thing is clear: in his *Passions of the Soul*, Article 34, Descartes says that 'the soul has its principal seat in the small gland located in the middle of the brain', and that 'the mechanism of our body is so constructed that simply by this gland's being moved in any way by the soul or by any other cause, it drives the surrounding spirits towards the pores of the brain, which direct them through the nerves to the muscles; and in this way the gland makes the spirits move the limbs' (Descartes, [1649] 1985, vol 1, p. 341). And in Article 41 he says that 'the activity of the soul consists entirely in the fact that simply by willing something it brings it about that the little gland to which it is closely joined moves in the manner required to produce the effect corresponding to this volition' (ibid., p. 343). It is clear that Descartes thinks of the relationship of the volition to the movement of the 'small gland' as causal, and of the relationship of the movement of the small gland to the movement (of the limbs) corresponding to the volition as causal.

What is not clear is whether he thinks of the relationship of the volition to the movement (of the limbs) corresponding to the volition as causal.

I am tempted to say, first, that he must think of it as causal, since if A causes B, and B causes C, it seems intuitively obvious that A causes C, and, secondly, that, even so, he does not think of it as causal in the Humian sense. Rather, he thinks of a volition as being related to its corresponding limb movement in something like the way in which O'Shaughnessy thinks of trying to raise a hand as being related to raising a hand. It is an 'internal' relationship. In other words, volitions are distinct from limb movements in the sense that they can *occur* without the corresponding limb movements, but not in the sense that they can be *specified* independently of the corresponding limb movements.

I am tempted to say this by Descartes' saying that there is a sense in which mind and body, despite being distinct substances, are united. In a letter to Princess Elizabeth of Bohemia, dated 21 May 1643, Descartes says that our notion of the soul's power to move the body depends on our having the notion of their union (Kenny, 1970, p. 138). It seems to me just possible (I put it no more strongly) that Descartes' statement that mind and body are united is his way of saying that when a man moves his hand voluntarily he moves his hand immediately (i.e. non-instrumentally), even though he is not immediately (i.e. non-inferentially) aware of moving it. In other words, willing is not something he does to bring about the movement of his hand as moving his hand is something he does to bring about the movement of a stone.

But if this is what Descartes meant to say then he certainly hit upon a paradoxical way of saying it, as he himself recognized. In a later letter to Princess Elizabeth, dated 28 June 1643, he wrote: 'It does not seem to me that the human mind is capable of conceiving at the same time the distinction and the union between body and soul, because for this it is necessary to conceive them as a single thing and at the same time to conceive them as two things; and this is absurd' (ibid., p. 142).

# 4 The Subordination of Agent Causation to Event Causation: Introspectionist Psychology

Descartes' remark that mind and body are united was not taken by other philosophers to be a concession to the Aristotelian view. Rather, it was taken to be a singularly unsuccessful attempt to explain how mind and body can interact. It was assumed that when Descartes talked about 'operations of the will' he meant that a voluntary movement is not a movement caused immediately by an *agent*, but is a movement caused by an *event*, the occurrence of an act of will in an agent.

If this standard interpretation of Descartes is correct, then from an Aristotelian point of view what Descartes did was to put an event causation construction on a fact of agent causation. In place of 'He raised his hand' Descartes would say 'He performed an act of will which (via events in the brain, nerves, and muscles) caused his hand to rise'. The fact that the first event in this event causation sequence, the 'operation of the will', is mental (meaning 'within us in such a way that we are immediately aware of it') does not alter the fact that in Descartes' philosophy a fact of agent causation has (in the words of Shakespeare's *Tempest*) suffered a sea-change into a fact of event causation.

The trouble is that if this move, this sea-change, is allowed to be made once, it is hard to stop it being made again, and again, and again. If it is allowed that voluntary movements are events caused by volitions then it is hard not to allow that volitions are caused by, say, motives, that motives are caused by character, and that character is caused by heredity and environment. The upshot is that agent causation comes to be regarded as an illusion, born of our ignorance of the chain of event causation that lies behind what we naively call 'our actions'.

Descartes restricted himself to the first move in this

subordination of agent causation to event causation. Voluntary movements are caused by volitions, but volitions are caused by men, not by events. In other words, *the will is free*. Descartes was most insistent on this. 'It is a supreme perfection in man that he acts voluntarily, that is, freely; this makes him in a special way the author of his actions and deserving of praise for what he does' (Descartes, [1644] 1985, vol. I, p. 205). Because our will is free, *we* are free; and 'there is nothing we can grasp more evidently or more perfectly' than our freedom (ibid., p. 206).

The subordination of agent causation to event causation was taken beyond Descartes' starting point by David Hume (1711–76). Descartes treated a voluntary movement as a movement caused by an event, the occurrence of an act of will, and stopped there. The will is free. Hume wanted to go further: to treat the act of will, also, as caused by an event. Preferably, it would be a mental event. We are, by definition, immediately aware of mental events. He needed (a) to think of something of which people are immediately aware (i.e. something mental) and which they already think of as having some connection with their actions, and (b) to produce a plausible explanation of how these mental events lead to acts of will and actions. Then he would have done for the mental world what Newton, with his theory of gravity (which explains why bodies move towards one another), had done for the natural world.

The materials were to hand. First, people habitually talk of 'motives' in connection with their actions. Secondly, if a person has a motive for acting in a certain way then he is immediately aware of it, just as he is immediately aware of his acts of will. Thirdly, John Locke, the doyen of British empiricist philosophers, had mentioned a psychological process, the 'association of ideas', which, with some modification, could be invoked to explain how particular motives lead to particular actions.

A modification was needed because Locke used the

expression 'association of ideas' in connection with an association that is out of the ordinary ('wholly owing to chance and circumstance'), whereas Hume wanted a theory that would explain what ordinarily happens, such as that people who are motivated by ambition act accordingly. Locke introduced 'the association of ideas' in the fourth edition (1700) of *An Essay concerning Human Understanding*, to describe such bizarre phenomena as that someone who had learnt to dance in a room in which there happened to be an old trunk might so connect being able to dance with the presence of the trunk that he could thereafter dance well only in a room containing that trunk or one like it (Locke, [1690] 1975, II.xxxiii.16). Hume, on the other hand, referred to 'the connexion or association of ideas' near the beginning of the first edition of *A Treatise of Human Nature* (Hume, [1739] 1978, I.i.4), and described it as 'a kind of ATTRACTION, which in the mental world will be found to have as extraordinary effects as in the natural, and to show itself in as many and as various forms' (ibid.). It was, for Hume, the explanatory principle *par excellence* for the workings of the mind, just as Newton's gravitational attraction was the principle for the workings of nature.

What is the relevance for the issue of agency and necessity of the association of ideas being like the gravitational attraction of planets? Hume gives the answer in a section of the *Treatise* entitled 'Of liberty and necessity':

> It is universally acknowledged that the operations of external bodies are necessary, and that in the communication of their motion, in their attraction, and mutual cohesion, there are not the least traces of indifference or liberty. Every object is determined by an absolute fate to a certain degree and direction of its motion, and can no more depart from that precise line, in which it moves, than it can convert itself into an angel, or spirit, or any superior substance. The actions, therefore, of matter are to be regarded as instances of necessary actions; and whatever is

in this respect on the same footing with matter, must be acknowledged to be necessary (ibid., II.iii.1).

According to Hume, mind is 'on the same footing with matter' in this respect. Just as the same events follow from the same causes in the natural world so the same motives always produce the same actions in the mental world (Hume, [1748] 1975, para 65). The science of mind is as deterministic as the science of nature.

Although Hume wanted there to be a science of mind distinct from the science of nature, he evidently thought of the association of ideas as being an effect, in the mental world, of something that happens in the natural world. What these physical causes may be, he says, 'I pretend not to explain' (Hume, [1739] 1978, I.i.4). He did, however, have recourse to physiology to explain mistakes in the association of ideas. It makes such fascinating reading that I make no apology for a long quotation:

> Twou'd have been easy to have made an imaginary dissection of the brain, and have shewn, why upon our conception of any idea, the animal spirits run into all the contiguous traces, and rouze up the other ideas that are related to it. But tho' I have neglected any advantage, which I might have drawn from this topic in explaining the relations of ideas, I am afraid I must here have recourse to it, in order to account for the mistakes that arise from these relations. I shall therefore observe, that as the mind is endow'd with a power of exciting any idea it pleases; whenever it dispatches the spirits into that region of the brain, in which the idea is plac'd; these spirits always excite the idea, when they run precisely into the proper traces, and rummage that cell, which belongs to the idea. But as their motion is seldom direct, and naturally turns a little to the one side or the other; for this reason the animal spirits, falling into the contiguous traces, present other related ideas in lieu of that, which the mind desir'd at first to survey. This change we are not always sensible of; but continuing still the same train of thought, make use of the related idea, which is presented to us, and employ it in our

reasoning, as if it were the same with what we demanded. This is the cause of many mistakes and sophisms in philosophy; as will naturally be imagin'd, and as it wou'd be easy to shew, if there was occasion (ibid., I.ii.5).

David Hartley (1705–57), whose *Observations on Man, His Frame, His Duty and His Expectations* was published in 1749, a year after Hume's first *Enquiry*, went further than Hume in his theorizing about the physiological basis of the association of ideas. According to Hartley, sensations in the mind are caused by vibrations occurring on the surface of the nerves and in the brain. Ideas of sensations correspond to the diminutive vibrations that are the vestiges of these vibrations. These diminutive vibrations become associated by joint occurrence, so that the occurrence of one predisposes another to occur. The association of ideas is the representation in the mind of this association of diminutive vibrations in the brain (Hartley, [1749] 1834; in Brown, 1970, p. 10).

John Stuart Mill agreed that we know that sensations are caused by 'some affection of the portion of our frame called the nervous system', but said that that is all we know. It is extremely probable that every mental state is the effect of a nervous state, but 'every one must admit that we are wholly ignorant of the characteristics of these nervous states'. Our only mode of studying them is by observing the mental states of which they are supposed to be the causes, and this, he says (in 1843), will be so 'for a long time at least, if not always'. The order of our mental phenomena must be studied in the mental phenomena themselves. It cannot be inferred from the laws of any phenomena more general. Therefore, he says, 'there is a distinct and separate Science of Mind' (Mill, [1843] 1974, VI.iv.2).

# 5 The Demise of Associationism

John Stuart Mill advocated 'a distinct and separate Science of Mind' – distinct and separate, that is, from the science of physiology. Its laws are those of the association of ideas, as propounded by Hume, by Hartley and, in particular, by John Stuart Mill's father, James Mill (1773–1836) in the latter's *Analysis of the Phenomena of the Human Mind* (Mill, [1829] 1869). In his father's book, J. S. Mill said, 'the principal laws of association, along with many of their applications, are copiously exemplified, and with a masterly hand' (Mill, [1843] 1974, VI.iv.3). In later editions of his *Systems of Logic*, Mill has a footnote at this point:

> When this chapter was written, Professor Bain had not yet published even the first part ('The Senses and the Intellect') of his profound Treatise on the Mind. In this the laws of association have been more comprehensively stated and more largely exemplified than by any previous writer; and the work, having been completed by the publication of 'The Emotions and the Will', may now be referred to as incomparably the most complete analytical exposition of the mental phenomena, on the basis of a legitimate induction, which has yet been produced.

Mill evidently expected Bain's 'comprehensive statement' of the laws of association to help associationist psychology on its way. But in fact the reverse happened. When a doctrine is stated clearly and unambiguously any faults there may be in it become apparent. Bain stated one of the laws of association, the 'law of contiguity' as follows: 'Actions, sensations and states of feeling, occurring together or in close connection, tend to grow together, or cohere, in such a way that, when any one of them is afterwards presented to the mind, the others are apt to be brought up in idea' (Bain, 1855, p. 327). To this, F. H. Bradley, the severest philosophical critic of associationism in the nineteenth century, objected that actions, sensations and states of feeling are particular experiences or events and cannot recur at all. They endure only for a fleeting moment, and

> they can never have more than one life; when they are dead they are done with. There is no Hades where they wait in disconsolate exile, till Association announces resurrection and recall. When the fact is bodily buried in the past, no miracle opens the mouth of the grave and calls up to the light a perished reality, unchanged by the processes that rule in nature. These touching beliefs of a pious legend may babble in the tradition of a senile psychology, or contort themselves in the metaphysics of some frantic dogma, but philosophy must register them and sigh and pass on (Bradley, 1883, p. 280, cf. pp. 287–9).

The 'frantic dogma' is the empiricist dogma that since an *I*, or agent, is not empirically discoverable, there is no *I*, or agent. The mind is simply a succession of perceptions, feelings, or states of mind, with no one in charge, so to speak. The 'senile psychology' is what Bradley elsewhere calls 'psychological Atomism' (ibid., p. 276), a theory that owes much to David Hume, and is described by the Humian philosopher Thomas Brown (1778–1820) in his *Lectures on the Philosophy of the Human Mind* (1820) as follows:

> If the mind of man, and all the changes which take place in it, from the first feeling with which life commenced to the last with which it closes, could be made *visible* to any other thinking being, *a certain series of feelings alone*, that is to say, a certain number of successive states of the mind, would be distinguishable in it, forming, indeed, a variety of sensations, and thoughts, and passions, as momentary *states* of the mind, but all of them existing individually, and successively to each other (Brown, 1970, p. 336).

Bradley's concern is with inference. He rejects psychological atomism because it is incompatible with any 'tolerably accurate theory of reasoning' (Bradley, 1883, p. 273). Briefly, it cannot accommodate someone to be responsible for the reasoning.

Our concern here is with agency. The psychological atomist construes a person's motive in doing something as a state of mind which precedes another state of mind, an act of will. He says that the same motives are always followed by the same actions. A defender of the notion of agency will reject this as giving an inaccurate picture of how motives are in fact related to actions. This objection was voiced in the eighteenth century by Abraham Tucker (1705–74) in *The Light of Nature Pursued*, a book he began writing in about 1756, seven years after the publication of David Hartley's *Observations on Man*. Tucker took an example from the poem *The Rape of the Lock* (1712–14) by Alexander Pope (1688–1744), and wrote:

To prevent mistakes, when I speak of the efficacy of motives and of their moving the mind to exert herself, I desire it may be understood that these are figurative expressions; and I do not mean thereby to deny the efficacy of the mind, or to assert any motion, force, or impulse imparted to her from the motives, as there is to one billiard ball from another upon their striking; but only to observe that motives give occasion to the mind to exert her endeavours in attaining whatever they invite her to, which she does by her own inherent activity, not by any power derived from them. And all mankind understand the matter so, except perhaps some few persons of uncommon sense and superfine understandings. When the poet makes Belinda ask, What mov'd my mind with youthful lords to roam? would he have you believe that vanity, pleasure, desire of conquest, hope of an advantageous match, or any other motive you can assign, made all those motions contained in the idea of roaming? No, surely – it was the lady herself by her own vigour and sprightliness. When she sits down to her toilet, unnumbered treasures ope at once. What opes the treasures? Why the maid, with her hands, not with her desire of tiffing out her mistress in a killing attire. And it is this agency of the mind which denominates an action ours, for whatever proceeds from other efficient causes does not belong to us . . .

Nobody will deny that we sometimes act upon motives, that we follow where they lead us, and that we should have acted otherwise had they not presented or had other motives appeared in the opposite scale to outweigh them . . .

But we run into frequent mistakes concerning the operations of motives, for want of first settling accurately with ourselves what they be. A motive I conceive is the prospect of some end actually in view of the mind at the time of action and urging to attain it (Tucker, [1768] 1834, vol. 1, ch. V, in Brown, 1970, pp. 104–5).

The difference between Hume and Hartley, on the one hand, and Tucker, on the other, could not be more marked. Hartley, following Hume's remark that 'the same motives always produce the same actions' (Hume, [1748] 1975, para. 65), says that 'motives seem to act like all other causes . . . so that where the motives are the same, the actions cannot be different, when the motives are different, the actions cannot be the same' (Brown, 1970, p. 85).

Tucker, on the other hand, distinguishes between the kind of causation involved in one billiard ball imparting motion to another upon their striking, and the kind involved in someone, Belinda, performing some action (roaming with youthful lords) from 'vanity, pleasure, desire of conquest, hope of an advantageous match, or any other motive you can assign'. It is precisely because motives do *not* 'act like all other causes' that it is false that 'where the motives are the same, the actions cannot be different, where the motives are different, the actions cannot be the same'. There *can* be different actions with the same motive (the 'youthful lords' may do any number of different things to win Belinda's heart) and the same action *can* be performed from different motives (roaming with youthful lords from vanity, pleasure, etc.) because someone doing something from a motive is *not* like a billiard ball being impelled to move by another billiard ball striking it; it is 'the prospect of some end actually in view of the mind at the time of action and urging to attain it'.

Hume and Hartley seem to have turned a blind eye to how we actually use the word 'motive'. Why?

The answer, I think, is that they were writing at a time when certain sorts of explanation were regarded as properly scientific, and other sorts were not. Explanations in terms of ends were not regarded as properly scientific. To understand how this came about we need to go back to Aristotle. Aristotle distinguished between two kinds of explanation of something happening. (Actually he distinguished between more than two, but it is only two of them that we need consider here.) One kind of explanation of something happening is in terms of an end for the sake of which it happens. Aristotle sometimes calls this 'final cause explanation'; it is also called 'teleological explanation' (from the Greek, *telos*, end, and *logos*, discourse or doctrine). The other kind of explanation of something happening is that it follows necessarily on something else happening; it happens, as Aristotle puts it, 'of necessity'. Sometimes Aristotle contrasts 'final cause' with 'motor cause'. Another term that is used is 'efficient cause'.

Aristotle regarded final cause explanation as more truly scientific than motor cause explanation. He wrote: 'That cause is the first which we call the final one. For this is the Reason, and the Reason forms the starting point, alike in the works of art and in the works of nature' *(On the Parts of Animals*, 639b14).

He considers a difficulty in the way of his doctrine that the final cause is the first: 'Why should not nature work, not for the sake of something, nor because it is better so, but just as the sky rains, not in order to make the corn grow, but of necessity? *(Physics*, 198b18).' In particular, why should it not be the case that things which clearly serve a purpose – for example, our front teeth being sharp, fitted for tearing, and our molars broad, useful for grinding – have become so as a result of the survival of the fittest? Aristotle clearly thinks we have to make a choice here. Either nature works for the sake of something, or it works of necessity; it cannot be the case that it works for the sake of something *and* does so because of what happens of necessity. A teleological explanation is, for him, a real explanation; it is not merely a way of describing facts that could equally well be described in non-teleological language.

All this is connected with his concept of *nature*. I referred, earlier, to Plato's two kinds of causes. On the one hand, there are things 'which are endowed with mind and are the workers of things fair and good'. On the other, there are things like fire and water, earth and air, 'things which, being moved by others, are compelled to move others'. In Aristotle's scheme of things there is also Nature, with a capital 'N'. Aristotle's 'Nature' has a peculiar status: it might be described as a mongrel concept. 'Nature' is like things 'endowed with mind' and yet not like them. Like things endowed with mind it acts for ends. Unlike things endowed with mind it cannot be asked why it does what it does, at least in the literal sense in which Socrates can be asked why he is sitting down. Moreover, its ends are unchanging. One can argue with Socrates, trying to get him to change his mind. But a thing of a certain natural kind, such as an acorn, has its future mapped out for it. It is of its essence that it should, if allowed to grow, become an oak and not an ash.

That there is such a thing as Nature, so described, is something Aristotle regards as proved by the fact that things do in fact work in such a way that ends are attained. He concludes, from the fact of there being ends to which motions tend, that 'there must be something or other really existing, corresponding to what we call by the name of Nature' (*On the Parts of Animals*, 641b26). In short, Nature really is purposive.

It might be supposed that Aristotle would attempt teleological explanations only in, say, biology. Teleological explanations are given in biology nowadays. For example, if the question is asked 'Why do the leaves of plants turn to face the sun?' an acceptable answer is 'In order to facilitate the process of photosynthesis whereby plants form carbohydrates from carbon dioxide and water'. It might be supposed that Aristotle would not look for teleological explanations in, say, astronomy. Not so. He writes:

> . . . we are inclined to think of the stars as mere bodies or units, occurring in a certain order but completely lifeless; whereas we ought to think of them as partaking of life and initiative. Once we do this, the events will no longer seem surprising . . . With these considerations in mind, we must suppose the action of the planets to be analogous to that of animals and plants (*On the Heavens*, 292a14–292b27).

Partly because the Aristotelian view of nature was recognized by the Church as being congenial to Christian faith, it, and the associated philosophy of science, survived for many centuries. In fact it was not until the first half of the seventeenth century that the study of 'final causes' gave way to that of 'motor causes'. Scientists and philosophers like Galileo (1564–1642) and Gassendi (1592–1655) ridiculed the Aristotelian philosophy (Galileo, [1623] 1957; Gassendi, [1624] 1959); and scientists, at their peril, started looking for mechanisms, not ends. In 1632 Galileo's *Dialogue Concerning the Two Chief World Systems – Ptolemaic and Copernican* (1953) was published. When it was realized that it was in fact a defence of the Copernican system, he was prosecuted for heresy and spent the last eight years of his life under house arrest.

Like Galileo and Gassendi, Descartes rejected Aristotelian teleology, but to avoid laying himself open to the sort of charges that were levelled against Galileo, he presented his philosophy, in the *Meditations*, as a demonstration of the existence of God, and the distinction between mind and body. It was only in private correspondence with the compiler of the *Objections* to the *Meditations*, Marin Mersenne, that he wrote, on 28 January 1641:

> I may tell you, between ourselves, that these six *Meditations* contain all the foundations of my *Physics*. But please do not tell people, for that might make it harder for supporters of Aristotle to approve them. I hope that readers will gradually get used to my principles, and recognize their truth, before they notice that they destroy the principles of Aristotle (Kenny, 1970, p. 94).

Nevertheless there are a few isolated passages in Descartes' published work in which his opposition to teleology is unequivocal. In his Fourth Meditation he wrote: 'I consider the customary search for final causes to be totally useless in physics' (Descartes, [1641] 1985, vol. II, p. 39), and in his reply to the Fifth set of *Objections* he said that conjectures as to what purpose God may have had in mind in his direction of the universe are futile in physics (ibid., p. 258).

The sort of explanation that was looked to as a paradigm of mechanical explanation in the new non-teleological physics was that provided by Isaac Newton (1642–1727), the explanation of the motions of material bodies in terms of the gravitational attraction they exert on one another. Accordingly, when philosophers, impressed by the successes of the new physics, turned their attention to explaining the workings of the mind, they looked for something analogous, in the mental world, to bodies in the natural world, and for something analogous, in the mental world, to gravitational attraction in the natural. Descartes conveniently provided them with the mental analogues of bodies in 'ideas', and Hume, adapting Locke's notion of the association of ideas to the purpose, did the rest: 'Here is a kind of ATTRACTION, which in the mental world will be found to have as extraordinary effects as in the natural' (Hume, [1739] 1978, I.i.4). The possibility of a reputable science of mind seemed to require that we should think of ideas as following necessarily on other ideas. Under the circumstances it is not surprising that motives, final causes if ever there were any, came to be thought of as 'the mechanical causes of actions' (Hartley [1749] in Brown, 1970, p. 86). It is not surprising that Hume and Hartley should have turned a blind eye to how we actually use the term 'motive'. It is not surprising that Tucker's plea that we should first settle accurately with ourselves what motives may be should go unheeded. Too much seemed to be at stake: the very possibility of a truly scientific (that is, non-teleological) psychology.

## 6 The Subordination Continued: Behaviourist Psychology and Physical Determinism

By the end of the nineteenth century practising psychologists had come to feel that they were engaged in a science that had separated off from speculative philosophizing and become a science in its own right. Wilhelm Wundt (1832–1920) founded the first laboratory of experimental psychology at Leipzig as early as 1870. It is hardly surprising that when philosophers, like F. H. Bradley in *The Principles of Logic* (1883), questioned the philosophical basis of introspectionist associationism, they were largely ignored. Too much had been invested to give up just because of a philosophical problem about how sensations and images can be said to recur.

Introspectionist associationism might have survived had it not been for two extraneous factors. The first was the inability of introspectionists to agree amongst themselves. One famous disagreement concerned the possibility of 'imageless thought'. Imageless thought is thinking that makes no use of images. Psychologists like Wundt and E. B. Titchener (1867–1927) held all mental processes to be constituted of sensations and images. The members of the Würzburg School, however, insisted that they could find no images in their introspections when solving several different sorts of problems.

Another typical disagreement between introspectionists is reported by the historian of psychology, E. G. Boring:

> . . . there is always to be remembered that famous session of the Society of Experimental Psychologists in which Titchener, after a hot debate with Holt, exclaimed: 'You can see that green is neither yellowish nor bluish!' and Holt replied: 'On the contrary, it is obvious that a green is that yellow-blue which is exactly as blue as it is yellow' (Boring, 1950).

Both these examples of disagreement illustrate the intrinsic weakness of introspectionism. So long as introspectionists agree about what they discover when they look into their minds all is well. But once they disagree, there seems to be no way of settling the disagreement.

The second extraneous factor was success in another field of investigation, the investigation of animal behaviour, to test Darwin's theory of the continuity between animals and man. The mode of observation used was, of course, that used in such sciences as zoology and biology – ordinary sense perception. Not only were the observations yielding results on which the investigators could agree; some of the theories to account for what was observed could even be tested under laboratory conditions.

Given the difficulty of settling disagreements when the method of observation is introspection, and the fruitfulness of the study of animals by ordinary observational methods, it is understandable that the thought should occur to psychologists that the same observational methods that were used in the study of animals might be used in the study of humans. In short, why not change psychology from being the study of the working of human *minds* to being the study of human (and animal) *behaviour*?

The first self-styled behaviourist was J. B. Watson (1878–1958). His first statement of behaviourism was in an article 'Psychology as the behaviorist views it' (Watson, 1913), but his views were more fully developed in his book, *Behaviorism*, first published in 1924 (Watson, 1957). The influence on him of the fruitfulness of the animal studies inspired by Darwin's theories is apparent in a remark in his introduction to the book: 'Behaviorism, as I tried to develop it in my lectures at Columbia in 1912 and in my earliest writings, was an attempt to do one thing – to apply to the experimental study of man the same kind of procedure and the same language of description that many research men had found useful for so many years in the study of animals lower than man' (ibid., p. i). The appropriate 'language of description', Watson held, is that of 'stimulus and response': 'The rule, or measuring rod, which the behaviorist puts in front of him always is: Can I describe this bit of behavior I see in terms of "stimulus and response"? By stimulus we mean any object in the general environment . . . By response we mean anything the animal does . . . ' (ibid., p. 6). The significance of this being the appropriate language of description is that the psychologist can himself provide the stimulus: 'The interest of the behaviorist in man's doings is more than the interest of the spectator – he wants to control man's reactions as physical scientists want to control and manipulate other natural phenomena. It is the business of behavioristic psychology to be able to predict and to control human activity' (ibid., p. 11).

For behaviourism to be more than a battle-cry, some explanatory principle, linking stimulus and response, was needed which would serve behaviourism as the doctrine of the association of ideas had served introspectionism – though, hopefully, not subject to equally telling objections.

Oddly enough, Descartes has a place in the history of the discovery of such a principle. He had supposed there to be two quite different ways in which bodily movements may be caused. First, 'animal spirits' reaching the brain through sensory channels may automatically be *reflected* into motor channels, producing what we call 'involuntary' movements. Secondly, the soul, by willing, can make the part of the brain with which it is united move in the way requisite for producing the bodily movement aimed at in the volition. Such a movement is said to be 'voluntary' (Descartes, 1985, vol. I, pp. 139, 341, 343; vol. II, pp. 161–2).

The explanation of involuntary movements in terms of a reflection of animal spirits (a 'reflex') was built upon by Ivan Pavlov (1849–1936). Pavlov found that digestive secretions take place in a dog not only in response to food, but also in response to what he called a 'psychic stimulus', such as the sound of the rattling of dishes in the preparation of food. In other words, the dog could be 'conditioned' to respond, with digestive secretions, to a substitute stimulus. The response was a 'conditioned response' or 'conditioned reflex'.

Pavlov's discovery was seized upon by the new behaviourist psychologists. Instead of acquired associations of ideas there are acquired associations of physical stimuli and behavioural responses. But there are limitations to Pavlovian conditioning. As practised by Pavlov, it applies only in the sphere of the involuntary. It is a way of making an animal respond involuntarily in a certain way to something to which it would not naturally respond in that way. It can be extended to cover man. But it is not obvious how it can be extended to cover what really matters, the kind of human behaviour that is ordinarily regarded as voluntary.

A contemporary of Darwin, T. H. Huxley (1825–95), declared man to be a conscious automaton, saying that 'the feeling we call volition is not the cause of a voluntary act, but the symbol of that state of the brain, which is the immediate cause of that act' (Vesey, 1964, p. 142). Mind, the province of the introspectionist psychologist, is, he said, an 'epiphenomenon'. But this was metaphysics, not experimental psychology. In the way in which Pavlov could make an animal secrete digestive juices in response to a sound, Huxley could not make a human being perform a voluntary movement by doing something to the state of his brain. What is needed is not a metaphysical theory but a scientific one, testable experimentally and with implications for the control of human behaviour.

Once again, it was experimental work involving animals that suggested a way forward. E. L. Thorndike (1874–1949) had been studying the problem-solving behaviour of cats. If they are imprisoned in a cage, to escape from which they would have to, say, pull a piece of string, how do they learn to do this? He observed that a cat would do a great many different things spontaneously, and eventually hit on the one which had the effect that the door of the cage opened, upon which it would make its escape from the cage. The next time it would again engage in a variety of spontaneous acts, but this time might pull the string a bit sooner. The time taken from imprisonment to escape, he noticed, lessened only very gradually. He took this to mean that the cat did not have any 'insight' into what was needed, but that the learning process (if one can properly call it 'learning') was the gradual strengthening of a stimulus-response connection – the connection between the stimulus of being imprisoned in the cage and the response of pulling the string to open the door.

Thorndike described this as learning by 'trial and error', the successful 'try' being 'reinforced' (i.e. made more likely to occur, earlier on in an imprisonment, in the future) by its success in securing release. It was also described as 'instrumental learning' and as 'operant conditioning'. It is obvious why it should be called 'instrumental learning', since the string-pulling is clearly instrumental in securing the cat's release from the cage. It is not so obvious why it should be called 'operant conditioning'. An 'operant' is 'that which operates', and pulling the string operates the release mechanism, but why call it 'conditioning'? The explanation, I think, is that the psychologists engaging in this work wanted to assimilate the learning process to that studied by Pavlov, the point being that in the explanation of Pavlovian conditioning no reference is made to mentalistic concepts like reasoning and insight; everything happens automatically, so to speak. If instrumental learning is really just another kind of conditioning, then it is not merely unnecessary, but improper, to invoke mentalistic concepts.

It may be objected to the use of the expression 'operant conditioning' that it blinds us to two significant differences between instrumental learning and Pavlovian conditioning. First, whereas Pavlovian conditioning depends on there being a reflex response, such as the secretion of digestive juices, to a stimulus, food, instrumental learning, as described by Thorndike, depends on there being something an animal *does*, in a sense in which the secretion of digestive juices in its stomach is not something it does. There could not be such a thing as instrumental learning if all of an animal's 'behaviour' consisted of reflex responses to stimuli. There must be something an animal does of its own accord, such as pulling a piece of string, if the effect of the string-pulling, namely escape from imprisonment in a cage, is to 'reinforce' such behaviour. Without the original spontaneous behaviour there would be nothing to reinforce.

Secondly, calling instrumental learning 'conditioning' suggests that *no* instrumental learning takes place quickly, through the agent realizing why a particular action produced the desired result. Perhaps cats and pigeons do not reason things out, or have 'insights'; but it is simply false that humans do not. Even behaviourist psychologists sometimes reason things out and have insights. Indeed, it is hard to understand how they could understand talk of 'reasoning and insight', as they evidently do when they deny that the problem solving behaviour of the lower animals involves these 'mentalistic processes', unless they were acquainted with the processes in question.

I conclude from these considerations that the actual facts of instrumental learning do not warrant B. F. Skinner's charge against Plato and Aristotle that they committed a 'fatal flaw' in attributing human behaviour to an autonomous agent, with intentions, purposes, aims and goals (Skinner, 1973, pp. 12–14). Just as the introspectionist, David Hartley, misrepresented motives by describing them as 'mechanical causes' of actions (Brown, 1970, p. 10), so the behaviourist, Skinner, misrepresents instrumental learning by describing the conditions under which it occurs as 'conditioning'. Both Hartley and Skinner have the aim of presenting psychology as a science which has no use for the notion of agent causation. They see the attribution of behaviour to an agent as introducing an element of unpredictability into the situation: if agents are responsible for what they do, and can act freely, then what they do cannot be brought under universal laws, and you cannot have a science without universal laws. In the case of Skinner, calling the conditions under which instrumental learning takes place 'conditioning' implies that the conditioning, and not the agent, should be held responsible for the behaviour. I am reminded of Socrates' reply to the suggestion that he is sitting down, awaiting whatever penalty Athens has ordered, because his sinews by relaxing and contracting enable him somehow to bend his limbs: 'Fancy being unable to distinguish between the cause of a thing and the condition without which it could not be a cause!' (Plato, *Phaedo*, 99b). An animal, or human being, could not learn to escape from a cage by pulling a piece of string unless the string-pulling had the desired effect, and so 'reinforced' the necessary behaviour. That is the condition under which learning takes place. Fancy concluding that the animal, or human being, is not responsible for the necessary behaviour!

Now, if neither introspectionist nor behaviourist psychologists, except by misrepresenting the facts, can make it seem likely that the notion of agent causation has no proper application, what, if anything, would make this seem likely? An answer is suggested by what G. J. Warnock says in a paper on 'Actions and events' (Warnock, 1963). Agent causation, as I said earlier, is characterized by the agent's being at liberty to move or not. Suppose Smith kicks Jones on the shin; for him properly to be held morally responsible for Jones' pain it must be the case that he could have *not* kicked Jones on the shin (by, for example, keeping both his feet on the floor). Now, his action of kicking Jones on the shin involves certain motions of his foot. Suppose (a) that everything that happens in and to physical objects can be brought under a deterministic system of physical laws ('physical determinism'), and (b) that in this respect human bodies are just like any other physical objects. It would seem to follow that if it is physically determined that Smith's foot should come into contact with Jones' shin then at least it *cannot* be true that Smith kept both his feet on the floor. Warnock writes:

> It appears — indeed, surely it is obvious — that the narratives of the physical determinist will be compatible only with those accounts of what people do which are themselves compatible with matter moving in the way narrated: and though there may well be several alternative such accounts, there will certainly be *some* that won't do. But this seems to mean that, if the thesis of physical determinism is true, then there *are some* things which, in a given situation, a person could *not* have done — those things, namely, which are ruled out by the narrative of how matters moved. And this does not seem to leave us anything like as much *latitude* in our views about what people could have done as we want to have and as we ordinarily believe that we do have in fact (ibid., p. 77).

Warnock goes on to suggest that the situation is really rather worse than this:

> Given the physical set-up, nothing could have occurred except what did occur; that is, matter could have moved *only* as in fact it did move. Now what the man in question *did* is certainly not thus determined, but the question left open here is surely only this: what, given that matter so moved, *might the person have been doing*? Certainly there will be a variety of possible answers to this question. But it seems clear that the range of possibilities will not be *the same* as that which we should normally consider as possible answers to the question *what he could have done*. In accepting the thesis of physical determinism we have in effect confined ourselves to those descriptions of actions *only* which are compatible with matters moving in a certain way; and in any case, it is surely evident that the question what someone, whose limbs moved in a certain manner, might have been doing, is, though open enough, quite different in principle from any ordinary sense of the question, what he *could have done* (ibid., p. 78).

In short, the answer suggested by what Warnock says is that if physical determinism is true, then the notion of agent causation does not have anything like the application I have taken it to have.

## 7 Over to Antony Flew

If Warnock's reasoning is valid, then if I accept physical determinism as a true thesis, it would appear that I ought to renounce what I will, for the moment, call 'my belief in agent causation'.

This, as I see it, is the problem of agency and necessity.

I could go on straight away to say what my response is to the problem; but this would perhaps be a good place to conclude my opening contribution to this debate so as to give Antony Flew a chance to enter the discussion. He will, I hope, not only present the problem as he sees it, but also comment on my formulation of it. Then, provided we are within striking distance of one another on what the problem is, we can start exchanging solutions.

# A First Engagement

ANTONY FLEW

# 1 Starting from the Moral Sciences and their Putative Presuppositions

My sometime Christ Church colleague Jim Urmson used occasionally to indulge in a mischievous speculation. Suppose that one philosopher were to say to another, 'I agree'. This unprecedented tribute would, in all probability, be construed as an insult. So it is with trepidation, and begging Godfrey Vesey's indulgence, that I now make confession. For at this stage I see no possibility of really substantial disagreement – save perhaps with regard to issues broached in his section 6, 'The subordination continued: behaviourist psychology and physical determinism'. But there my remarks have to be reserved until after he has declared his own intentions.

Far from disagreeing with the main lines of his first contribution, I want to begin by stressing that I approve wholeheartedly of his presentation of our problems as today arising most urgently from what Hume would have called 'moral subjects'. Following a change in usage which has occurred in the years between, we might prefer to describe these not as moral subjects but as moral sciences. The word has, however, to be Hume's 'moral' rather than what is to us, in the relevant context, the more familiar 'social'. For we need a word to embrace not only history, sociology, economics, anthropology and the like, but also individual, even individualistic, non-social psychology, if such there can be.

Throughout the English-speaking world, and perhaps above all in Britain, this is a secular age. Nowadays the noisiest pronouncements even of ecclesiastical spokespersons preach a social gospel rather than any more traditional return to religion; which social gospel, it seems, is always semi-socialist, if not a complete 'liberation theology' of total and hence totalitarian socialism. For instance, at the time of writing, the British Council of

Churches, in a campaign generously financed by the charity Christian Aid, had as its sole message for travellers on the London Underground a summons to pray that the Marxist–Leninist regime in Nicaragua be left in peace. There was, significantly, no corresponding call for similar spiritual support for the at least equally harassed but Christian-Democratic government of El Salvador.

It is, therefore, for better or for worse, far easier to excite most of our contemporaries about the secular question – whether the presuppositions and the findings of the moral sciences can be reconciled with our everyday assumption that, as agents, we always can, in some profound sense, do other than we do do. The parallel but different religious problem is whether the creatures of a Creator could be sufficiently autonomous to be justly accountable for their deeds; and justly accountable, above all, to such a continuously manipulative God. Nor could we have found clearer or more suitably provocative statements from which to start than those provided by B. F. Skinner. Besides, they come to us with the academic authority of a senior Harvard professor – the acknowledged doyen of all behaviouristic psychology. Also, they have had, through best-selling books, wide distribution and much public attention.

Vesey takes his quotations from what Skinner saw as his last testament; but the same doctrines are propounded in earlier works. Thus, in *Science and Human Behavior*, we can read: 'The hypothesis that man is not free is essential to the application of scientific method to the study of human behavior' (Skinner, 1953, p. 447). The point is made again, in a more popular way, by the same author's mouthpiece in a utopian novel: 'I deny that freedom exists at all. I must deny it – or my programme would be absurd. You can't have a science about a subject matter which hops capriciously about' (Skinner, 1948, ch. XXIX). Again, under that sinister yet altogether appropriate title *Beyond Freedom and Dignity*, Skinner argues in his own person: 'Two features of autonomous man are particularly troublesome. In the traditional view, a person is free. He is autonomous in the sense that his behaviour is uncaused. He can therefore be held responsible for what he does, and justly punished if he offends' (Skinner, 1971, 1972, p. 19; compare Flew, 1978, ch. 7).

There are two points to be made about this at once. First, as comes out more clearly from passages already quoted by Vesey, Skinner is inclined to assume that in 'the pre-scientific view' human behaviour has to be attributed to an 'indwelling agent'. Certainly this is true of Plato who, above all in *Phaedo*, insists that, as rational and responsible agents, we all of us essentially are incorporeal souls; souls somehow resident, not to say imprisoned, in the bodies we control. But this, as Vesey's later references make clear, was equally certainly not the view of Aristotle. He did not hypothesize an incorporeal or even a corporeal 'indwelling agent'. For him – as, surely, in truth – the human agents were and are the flesh and blood people themselves.

It is for many purposes fruitful to see Plato and Aristotle as the Founding Fathers of two rival traditions about the nature of man: the Platonic, or Platonic–Cartesian, holding that the human essence is incorporeal, and that it could significantly be said to exist separately either after the dissolution or even before the beginning of its body; the Aristotelian maintaining that human beings simply are a (very special) kind of creature of flesh and blood, with the usually unstated implication that it makes no sense even to suggest that a personality might precede the conception, or survive the death and dissolution, of the person of whom it is the personality (Flew, 1964, Introduction).  ·

Skinner's false assumption of a common and collective 'Greek view' must, nevertheless, be rated venial. For it is one too often encouraged, or even maintained, by people paid both to know and to do better. Chisholm (1963), for instance, begins with the motto: ' "A staff moves a stone, and is moved by a hand, which is moved by a man", Aristotle, *Physics*, 256a.' Yet the philosopher author has insisted on entitling his paper 'Human Freedom and the

Self', a title which, to anyone able to guess the intended referent in that peculiar and unexplained technical usage, will suggest a Platonic 'indwelling agent', an incorporeal soul.

Before proceeding to the second point about Skinner, I take Chisholm's motto as my cue to answer the question raised about the case of the man with the anaesthetized arm reported by William James and discussed by Vesey on pp. 13ff. I agree with Vesey that we ought here to follow Aristotle, by saying that it seemed to this patient 'as if he raised his hand (apart from his not feeling it rise), but in fact he did not do anything'. It would, surely, be correct to speak of trying, and failing, only where the patient is aware of making an unusual effort, but still not succeeding? Suppose, for instance, that he knew that his arms had been paralysed as a result of some injury, but that now, after a spell in hospital, he was making a big effort to recover their normal use.

Also, Vesey's treatment of basic actions may perhaps be reinforced usefully by two further remarks. First, the question 'How?' put of any basic action has to be construed as asking for an adverbial answer: not 'How (by what means'?); but 'How (in what manner)?'. Second, the intended production of any psychokinetic effect, or of any other genuine psi-phenomenon, must necessarily constitute a basic action: for the use of means is here ruled out by definition (Flew, 1987).

There is a second point about Skinner's *Beyond Freedom and Dignity* which, while we are indicating the more than merely academic relevance and importance of the issues under discussion, needs to be emphasized heavily. It is that the repudiation of what is in his eyes the black beast notion of 'autonomous man' leads Skinner, very reasonably, to put little or no value upon political liberty. Thus he refuses to recognize any significant difference between a set-up in which abortion is illegal and one in which it is not. In the latter case, he says, with a perverse sneer: 'The individual is "permitted" to decide the issue for himself [sic!], simply in the sense that he will act because of consequences to which legal punishment is no longer to be added' (Skinner, 1973, p. 97). Well, yes, I suppose, precisely in that sense; for exactly that is what it is all about. Skinner has already shown the same doctrinally determined scotoma with regard to the difference between having or not having criminal laws forbidding people to 'gamble, drink, or go to prostitutes' (ibid., p. 91).

Again, he considers 'the practice of inviting prisoners to volunteer for possibly dangerous experiments — for example, on new drugs — in return for better living conditions or shorter sentences'. He asks, rhetorically, 'But are they really free when positively reinforced . . . ?' (ibid., p. 39). Since positive reinforcement is precisely and only his fancy way of referring to the promised rewards, the correct answer is, clearly, 'Yes'. The contrast is, for instance, with those prisoners in Belsen and Dachau who were made subjects for medical experimentation willy nilly. (For a more thorough examination of the political implications of Skinner's ideas, compare Flew, 1978. The three Marxist critics quoted by Vesey must have found this aspect congenial, dissenting only in their insistence that the elite to be established in irremovable despotic power must be, as Skinner's is not, Leninist.)

If we were considering questions about whether people are or are not, or ought or ought not to be, at liberty to do or not to do something, then what we would be asking is whether they are, or ought to be, constrained to do, or restrained from doing, that particular something. That would then be 'exactly . . . what it is all about'. Such questions of political liberty may well become properly important only in so far as Skinner's denial of the reality of 'autonomous man' is itself denied. But although or, rather, because the two kinds are thus connected, we must insist that it is wrong to identify, on the one hand, questions about acting of one's own freewill as opposed to acting under some sort of constraint, and, on the other hand, questions about the presuppositions, nature and implications of agency. That is why the title of the present book is not 'Freewill and Necessity' but 'Agency and Necessity'.

This distinction between the two kinds has often been collapsed, or not made; and both these sins, sins of commission and of omission, are common still. They were the objects of Locke's rebuke when he wrote in the *Essay*: 'I think the question is not proper, *whether the will be free*, but *whether a man be free*' (II.xxi.21). Yet a recent writer, whose work was selected for inclusion in an Oxford anthology, announced, apparently without hesitation: 'It seems to be generally agreed that the concept of free will should be understood in terms of the *power* or *ability* of agents to act otherwise than they in fact do. To deny that men have free will is to assert that what a man *does* do and what a man *can* do coincide' (van Inwagen, 1982, pp. 49–50). Although, as an account of the ordinary meaning of the expression in question, this is irredeemably erroneous, it would, it may be admitted, serve quite well as an explanation of one essential element in agency.

It is impossible to be similarly charitable towards two subsequent offerings from the same writer, for van Inwagen proceeds in short order first, to express his contempt for the contentions that the meanings of 'of their own free will' and of associated expressions can be elucidated, and can be shown to have actual application, by reference to accepted paradigm cases (ibid., pp. 55–6); and then, with an equally supercilious confidence, he offers an erroneous definition of 'predestinarianism'.

Predestinarians, he informs us, maintain two propositions: '(i) that if an act is foreseen it is not free, and (ii) that all acts are foreseen by God' (ibid., p. 56). All this, as will soon be shown by quotation from some of the classical theologians, displays a simple ignorance. For those great, yet no doubt fundamentally misguided thinkers, made so bold as to hold both that many of our actions can in truth be said to be performed freely, and that not only these and all other actions, but also all other events, are not merely foreseen, but foreordained, and ultimately caused, by God.

The last three paragraphs of the previous discussion have pointed out some popular misconceptions. This exercise has here a twofold purpose. The first is correction: these are all misconceptions against which those embarking upon discussion of the present topic require to be warned. The second is support. We have here a second methodological matter upon which Vesey and I are in strong agreement. It is that in such discussions we should always remember various relevant arguments, distinctions and objections which were urged, made, or put by the great men of old. None of these contributions – nor, for that matter, anything else – is to be accepted uncritically. But neither are they to be merely ignored. We cannot hope to make solid and substantial progress in philosophy unless we are ever ready to learn from our predecessors.

Far too many philosophers, not only amateurs but professionals also, have seemed and still do seem to be strenuously striving to obey an anti-Puritan maxim; a maxim which misguided the student revolutionaries of the 1960s. It is: 'Live each day as if your first!' For instance: not all that long ago, whole new books used to be produced by authors apparently unaware that any respectable philosophers either had ever maintained or were still maintaining any position of the kind now – perhaps following an early initiative of mine – properly named 'compatibilist'. Compatibilists, called 'soft determinists' by William James, hold that philosophical diplomacy can, through modest modifications and mutual concessions, reconcile what are often thought to be the flat incompatible contentions of two camps formerly opposed.

Many classical philosophers – including Hobbes and, most famously, Hume – have been, in this understanding, compatibilists. So that is not a position to be dismissed without examination. So not to be aware that it has been, and still is, thus most respectably held is really to disqualify yourself from full participation in the present discussion. Since, in one form or another, that discussion has been going on more or less continuously since the time of Plato, there are by now quite a lot of distinctions, arguments and objections to which we may fairly apply a sharp remark which Hobbes made in his own 'great debate', his pamphlet war with Bishop Bramhall. Thomas Hobbes (1588–1679) said, of one particular crucial distinction, that anyone who was not seized of that difference 'is not fit . . . to hear this controversy disputed, much less to be a writer in it' (Hobbes, 1839–45, V, p. 51).

Vesey and I both hope that readers of the present book, even if they are not persuaded to agree with either of us on any substantive issue, will through that reading qualify not only 'to hear this controversy disputed', but also to participate themselves. I suggest that it was the failure, through neglect of such necessary propaedeutic study, to consolidate ground previously gained which in some significant part explains why Milton's highbrow Devils made no progress in their inquiries:

> Others apart sat on a hill retir'd,
> In thoughts more elevate, and reason'd high
> Of providence, foreknowledge, will, and fate,
> Fix'd fate, free will, foreknowledge absolute,
> And found no end, in wand'ring mazes lost.
>
> (*Paradise Lost*, II. 557–61)

## 2 Physical and Moral Causes: Getting the Distinction Right

Vesey in his section 2 starts from a fundamental distinction made very clearly by Plato. But to find labels for the elements in this distinction Vesey resorts to various philosophers writing in the 1960s, most of whom appear to have been unaware that they had been anticipated by any of the ancients. This innocence would have been of little moment had their independent work been better than, or even as good as, that of Plato. But to speak, as following (some of) them Vesey does, of 'agent causation and event causation' is bound to suggest that the distinction is between different sorts of causing rather than between different senses of (the word) 'cause'. The consequent confusion is most manifest in a statement by one member of this group of philosophers, who himself prefers a terminology even less satisfactory: 'I shall say that when one event or state of affairs (or set of events or states of affairs) causes some other event or state of affairs, then we have an instance of *transeunt* causation. And I shall say that when an *agent*, as distinguished from an event, causes an event or state of affairs, then we have an instance of *immanent* causation' (Chisholm, 1964, p. 28).

But suppose that some action of mine − pressing a plunger, for example − causes something to occur − the blowing of a bridge, say − then this cause is a cause in exactly the same sense, and is a cause of exactly the same sort, as the similarly forceful impact of some accidentally falling object striking a similar detonator similarly connected. Both these two causes − both the action, that is, and the event which is precisely not an action − make something happen. Both equally necessitate: both equally, that is to say, in consequence of their occurring in all the various circumstances given, make it (practically) inevitable that the same explosive effect should occur and (practically) impossible that it should not.

The enormously important difference, and hence the right distinction, lies between, on the one hand, the sense in which an agent is said *to be caused* to act, and, on the other hand, the sense in which anything else is said *to be caused* to occur. In the modern literature the earliest source providing an entirely satisfactory account of these two senses is R. G. Collingwood's *An Essay on Metaphysics*. The first is there defined as that in which 'that which is "caused" is the free and deliberate act of a conscious and responsible agent, and "causing" him to do it means affording him a motive for doing it'. In the second, 'that which is "caused" is an event in nature, and its "cause" is an event or state of things by producing or preventing which we can produce or prevent that whose cause it is said to be' (Collingwood, 1940, p. 285). (Since Vesey has quoted from Thorndike's account of what he calls 'trial and error learning', it becomes relevant to mention that in this book Collingwood developed a vehement, undeservedly neglected, and still by no means completely dated critique of rash theorizings by Thorndike and by several other leading experimental psychologists.)

It would be superfluous to provide a further illustration of the employment of the word 'cause' in that second, altogether familiar sense. But, although its use in the first sense is in fact equally familiar, emphatic reminders are as essential as they have been rare. So consider, for example, my hearing of the news that some favourite enemy has suffered a misfortune. I may choose to construe this as a cause for celebration. If I do, then it will be correct both for me and for everybody else to say that my hearing of this news was both my reason for celebrating and the cause of my celebration. Nevertheless, I was the agent in the whole business, not a patient. Nothing and no one compelled me to celebrate, to make whoopee willy nilly. I could instead – and, had I been a nicer person, perhaps I would – have taken the acquisition of exactly the same information as a cause for commiseration. Had I chosen to respond in this way, it would then have been correct, both for me and for everyone else, to say that my hearing of this same news was both my reason for commiserating and/or the cause of my commiserating. So we have here a kind of case in which the very same cause may have not merely a different but an opposite effect.

Let me, between parentheses, remark that one of the few philosophers still attending to Collingwood gets things badly twisted here: 'The root metaphor, . . . is that of a person bringing it about that another person . . . does something which the first person wishes to have done. It is worth noting, therefore, that that root metaphor is essentially that of compulsion' (Sellars, 1976, p. 142). Sometimes, when the reason provided for the second person to act as the first person wishes is a formidable threat, we do have a case of compulsion. But this is not so when – as in the case of the prisoner volunteers mentioned by Skinner – the reason is a promise of reward.

The previously explained difference between two senses of 'cause' is so great, and of such pervasive practical importance, that we must mark it in some memorable way. The example to follow is that of the idiomatic distinction between 'funny (ha ha)' and 'funny (peculiar)'. The problem is what to put between the brackets. In previous publications I proposed 'physical' and 'personal'. I now suggest that it is better to take a tip from Hume. He explains his way of making a distinction of this sort in one of his *Essays*. (These, unlike the *Treatise* and the *Enquiries*, are not much read by philosophers.)

Though compatible with and indeed complementary to our way of making such a distinction, his is quite different: 'By *moral* causes, I mean all circumstances, which are fitted to work on the mind as motives or reasons. . . . By *physical* causes I mean those qualities of the aire and climate, which are supposed to work insensibly on the temper, by altering the tone and habit of the body . . . (Hume, [1742] 1985, p. 198).' This specification assures that causes (moral) are, in Plato's words, 'endowed with mind', even if not always 'workers of things fair and good'. But it does not provide, as it should, for an essential element of practical necessity; for causes (physical) being, again in Plato's words, 'things which, being moved by others, are compelled to move others'. On the contrary, that is something which Hume wishes positively to deny; and which he must deny if his 'reconciling project' is to go through.

We shall come later to that compatibilist exercise. The immediate task is to bring out further implications and ramifications of this fundamental and seminal distinction between causes (moral) and causes (physical). Once it has been adequately drawn we see that we must also make, and be ever ready to employ, a parallel distinction between two kinds of determinism.

In a very widely circulated essay in the applied philosophy of history the author, himself a leading historian, gives what he assumes will be a generally acceptable definition of 'determinism'. With acknowledgements to the philosopher Samuel Alexander, this is said to be 'the belief that everything that happens has a cause or causes, and could not have happened differently unless something in the cause or causes had also been different' (Carr, 1961, p. 87).

So long, but only so long, as the word 'cause' is read in the physical sense, this passes. Certainly, too, if it is read in this way, then determinism is a doctrine of practical necessitation and practical inevitability. But if it is read in the moral sense – as, in the context of history and the other moral sciences it almost always ought to be – then we are, as Americans say, in an entirely different ball game. For to assert that all actions may be explained in terms of their moral causes – in terms, that is to say, of the agents' motives, purposes, intentions, and the like – is, precisely not to say that those agents were necessitated so to act; that all their actions were unavoidable even by the agents themselves. On the contrary, to maintain that Jack or Jill did this or that because they wanted to such and such is: not to imply that they could not have done otherwise; but to presuppose that they could. (For a critique of Carr's own treatment of these issues, compare Flew, 1978, ch. 3.)

It is scarcely possible to exaggerate the importance either of this distinction between two senses of 'cause', or of the parallel, derivative distinction between two senses of 'determinism'. Once we have got a grip on these, it becomes obvious that it is only determinism of the physical kind which presents a threat *Beyond Freedom and Dignity*. That is why this book bears its present title rather than 'Agency and Determinism'.

The well-nigh universal failure to make the second distinction gives rise to endless confusion; while that failure itself is in part to be accounted for by the fact that those who do make some distinction between physical and moral causes so often do this — as, we saw, did Hume — without noticing, or at any rate without emphasizing that, although the one sort necessitates, the other does not. This confusion pervades both the social sciences themselves and external interpretations of their significance.

For instance, in a commendably open-minded piece on *Thinking about Crime*, one author tosses off, as if it were totally undisputatious, the remark: ' . . . if causal theories explain why a criminal acts as he does, they also explain why he *must* act as he does . . . ' (Wilson, 1977, p. 63). So usual indeed is it to assume that finding the causes of human behaviour must always be a matter of finding factors that somehow necessitate that behaviour, that public tribute should be paid to those rare researchers who never for one moment either assume or suggest that all human beings must, or even will, respond to the same environmental stimuli in the same way. (See, for instance, Alice Coleman and others, 1985.)

Nor is the present lamentable situation likely to be much improved so long as the most frequently employed textbooks in the philosophy of the social sciences are works making nothing of these crucial distinctions. Such

books in consequence neglect even to raise the fundamental question whether there either are or could be laws
of nature physically determining, and so somehow necessitating, the senses of actions. (Compare Ryan, 1970;
Lessnoff, 1976; Pratt, 1978; and Papineau, 1978; but
contrast Flew, 1985.)

# 3 Physical and Moral Causes: Profiting from that Distinction

For our present purposes, the most interesting feature of all the consequent confusion is the mistaking of evidence for determinism (moral) to be evidence for a necessitating determinism (physical). This is something which, if you have discerned no relevant ambiguity in either of the two key terms, you are bound to do. And the name of those to whom these insights have not been vouchsafed is Legion. Freud, for instance, advocated, under the description 'psychic determinism', what in our terminology must be accounted a species of the genus determinism (moral). But he certainly saw this as the psychological special case of that general, ultra-hard, physical determinism in which – in the heyday of the great Vienna medical school – he had himself been raised (Flew, 1978, ch. 8–9). Yet, whatever the ultimate truth, the two should appear to be, immediately and at first sight, incompatible.

It has often been argued that if, and in so far as, all our actions are motivated, then to that extent we must be subject to a universal necessitating determinism. It can never be possible for us to do other than we do do. In the eighteenth century this argument is found, fully developed, in section V of Joseph Priestley's *The Doctrine of Philosophical Necessity Illustrated* (1777). In the nineteenth century Sir Francis Galton reached the same conclusion by the same road. He kept account in a notebook of occasions when he had made decisions believing that several alternative courses of action were equally open to him. But he always found, he thought, looking back, that he had had reasons sufficiently strong to determine that he would act – must have acted – in the sense in which in fact he had. In the same century Arthur Schopenhauer (1788–1860), quoting Priestley (1733–1804), followed the same path to the same conclusion (Schopenhauer, [1841] 1960, pp. 79–80).

In our own century the writings of Freud and his followers have been full of similar arguments. Ernest Jones, for instance, both a foundation member of the original Fellowship of the Ring and Freud's official biographer, dismissed certain 'psychological arguments against the belief in a complete mental determinism'. These, he urged, only show

> that the person is not aware of any conscious motive. When, however, conscious motivation is distinguished from unconscious motivation, this feeling of conviction teaches us that the former does not extend over all our motor resolutions. What is left free from the one side receives its motive from the other – from the unconscious – and so the psychical determinism is flawlessly carried through. A knowledge of unconscious motivation is indispensable, even for philosophical discussion of determinism (Jones, 1920, pp. 77–8).

I have argued elsewhere that unconscious and conscious motives relate to actions in different ways (Flew, 1978, ch. 8). But here the crucial point is that it is radically wrong to construe at any rate conscious desires as necessitating causes (physical). Whenever I want to do anything, which it is within my power to do, I can choose whether or not actually to do it. That indeed is what it means to say of human beings that things are within their powers (Flew, 1985, pp. 89–97). Desiring as such, therefore, never necessitates doing. It is always up to the agents which of their desires they adopt as their operative motives. When in one of Agatha Christie's always cunningly constructed detective stories Hercule Poirot asks who might have had a motive to murder, it frequently appears that this would be true of almost everyone in sight. Yet in the end it emerges that – usually – only one character did in fact (or in fiction) adopt the relevant desire as his or her motive for the actual murder.

To all this the stock reply contends that, if we do not act to satisfy one desire, then that is only because we are impelled by another and stronger, which demands and, if it is the stronger, necessarily achieves, satisfaction. Jonathan Edwards (1703–58), the first major philosophical talent to develop in territories which later became part of the USA, wrote, in his treatise on the *Freedom of Will*:

> And I think it must also be allowed by all, that everything that is properly called a motive ... has some sort and degree of tendency ... to excite the will, previous to the effect or to the act of the will excited. This previous tendency of the motive is what I call the 'strength' of the motive ... And in this sense, I suppose, the will is always determined by the strongest motive (Edwards, [1756] 1957, p. 142).

But neither Edwards himself, nor any of his successors, has ever been able to specify any way of identifying the stronger or the strongest desire without viciously circular reference to what the desiring agent does in fact eventually do. Nor will anyone else ever be able to turn this trick. For the very idea of a stronger or a strongest thus independently identifiable is grounded in the misconception that the logic of desire is that of a mechanical force. Could this impossible trick be turned it would become in principle possible for Poirot to discover murderers by detecting who had the stronger or the strongest of desires to kill the eventual victims. But the truth is that it cannot be done, and never will be.

The misconception that our desires are external forces pushing us, and pushing us where they rather than we will, is at least as old as classical mechanics. We cannot hope to demolish it in any way more effective or delightful than that of Abraham Tucker – in the paragraph about the maid in Pope's *The Rape of the Lock* 'tiffing out her mistress in a killing attire'; a passage which Vesey discovered and has shared with the rest of us in his first contribution (pp. 27–8).

What so many have wanted to do, and what some still hanker after doing, is to develop a science of individual psychology on the model of elementary physics. This would misconstrue our desires, in just this way, as external forces operating upon us; and show how our actual actions must be the inevitable resultants of the interplay upon our otherwise inert bodies of these external forces. Thus, in section IV of the treatise mentioned earlier, Priestley (1777) wrote: ' . . . opposite motives as causes of love and hatred are known to balance one another, exactly like weights in opposite scales. According to all appearance nothing can act more invariably or mechanically.' It helps too to introduce the popular pseudo-technical term 'drives', carrying the strong unwarranted suggestion of our being passively driven.

Notwithstanding its perennially seductive appeal this whole enterprise is altogether hopeless. Our desires, as we have just been reminding ourselves, simply are not *external forces*. Any of the desires which we happen to have we may or may not adopt as our motives for action; as we choose. Nor is any action which we choose to perform *necessitated* by the desire which we ourselves adopted as its motive. Nor, finally, does the vector analogy apply. For desires do not all and always exercise in determining a resultant action an influence precisely proportionate to their supposedly measurable strength. Often one or more is fully satisfied while others are frustrated totally.

Frequently, in concluding from the presence of powerfully explanatory motivation to (what is always taken to be) an inexorably necessitating and hence completely exculpatory determinism, a lot is made of two massively misleading idioms: 'he had no choice'; and 'she could not have done otherwise'. The crux is that the correct application for those common idioms is to cases where it is not to be denied, but taken for granted, that in a profounder sense, which it is a main task of the present book to explicate, the agents *did* have a choice, and *could* have done otherwise. Consider, for example, a second psychoanalytic statement. Conceding that everyone is sure that in unimportant decisions the agent can do either this or that 'as he wishes', the thesis is that: 'With vital decisions . . . it is characteristic that he feels irresistibly impelled towards one and one only, and that he really has no choice in the matter nor desires to have any. Luther's famous "Hier stehe Ich. Ich kann nicht anders" . . . is a classical example' (Jones, 1926, II, pp. 81–2). It is noteworthy that Freud himself had employed this same illustration, and misunderstood it in the same way (Freud, 1901, pp. 253–4).

These most famous words of the archetypal Protestant hero are not, however, to be interpreted, as the French would say, 'at the foot of the letter'. Luther was not claiming to have fallen victim to a sudden general paralysis. For to say, in the everyday sense of 'could have done otherwise', that I could not have done otherwise, is not merely not inconsistent with but actually presupposes the truth of the assumption that, in a more fundamental sense, I could. What, as really we all know, Luther meant – and indeed said – was: not that he was afflicted with a general paralysis, and hence unable to withdraw; but that none of the alternative courses of action open to him were, to him, acceptable.

Again, consider people who, unlike Luther before the Diet of Worms, act not of their own free will but under compulsion. It may be the bank manager who opens the safe and hands out its contents in face of the threatening machine guns of Mr 'Legs' Diamond and his business associates. Or it may be a small girl who says something rude to her teacher because a horrid boy threatened to spoil her pretty new frock if she did not. The excuse that they acted under compulsion does not imply that there was no alternative possible course of action which they might have chosen. There was in each case a very obvious alternative available. It is precisely that alternative to which their respective excuses refer. The point is, not that the agent had no alternative, but that, although there was an alternative, it was one which the agent could not properly be blamed or punished for not choosing.

Both the person who does something of his own free will, and the person who does the same thing under compulsion, act. There therefore must have been some alternative which they might have chosen. It is for this reason, and for this reason only, reasonable that we should – as we do – require more formidable alternatives to excuse more serious offences. Had our bank manager been able to plead only that 'Legs' Diamond had threatened to spoil his, the manager's, natty executive suit, his excuse would, even in our soft and permissive period, have been unacceptable. Such differentiation would be unwarranted and unintelligible if those pleading that they acted only under compulsion had in truth not acted at all; if really, in the more fundamental senses, they had had no choice and could not have acted otherwise.

For there is no doubt but that cases where people act, or refrain from acting, under compulsion are totally different from cases where they do not act at all. Suppose that I am overpowered by a team of skilful strong-arm men, who throw me willy nilly out of the window. Suppose too in consequence that I fall through the roof of your greenhouse, and that your treasured orchids are ruined by that fall. Then, however excusable in the excitement of the moment, it would be incorrect for you to demand to know why I did such damage to those precious orchids, or for me to explain that I acted only under compulsion. For there is no conduct of mine to be explained or excused. I did not do or refrain from doing anything. I did not act under compulsion. I did not act at all. The responsible agents were the defenestrators. I was simply a missile victim.

Luther before the Diet of Worms, and anyone else in a similar predicament, would at one time have been described as being subject to a 'moral necessity' to do what he did. The adjective is acceptable, provided that it is employed in the sense explained above, as the opposite of 'physical'. But the noun, in as much as it suggests and presumably is intended to suggest that the persons concerned are not truly agents able to do other than they do do, is diametrically wrong.

Jonathan Edwards was at his best in treating this topic. His account of how, as flesh and blood people, we all can and do, from our everyday experience of the realities, acquire the idea of (what he called natural rather than) physical necessity is something which must have been intended – to mix the language of old-time pamphleteers and contemporary commercial advertisers – as a personalized cooling card for Hume. For Hume was officially committed to denying both that we can have any legitimate idea of, and that there is, any such thing. That 'officially' requires heavy emphasis. For, except when directly discussing this thus disputed notion and its possible application, Hume is at least as ready as the next man to assert that natural necessities do in fact obtain. The passage which Vesey quoted earlier (pp. 22–3) will do second service by confirming this claim.

We may at the same time, before returning to Edwards, refer to, and point a relevant moral to be drawn from, Vesey's subsequent treatment of Hume's ' "frantic dogma" . . . that . . . the mind is simply a succession of perceptions, feelings, or states of mind, with no one in charge, so to speak' (p. 26). For it is because he insists on asking only what experience would be available to such an incorporeal not-subject, forever disqualified from any discovering through doing, that Hume is destined to conclude that we do not have experience, and therefore cannot have a legitimate idea, of physical necessity (Hume, [1739] 1978, I.iii.14; and compare Flew, 1986, ch. V–VI).

To this day it is common for philosophers – even philosophers who may think of themselves as having decisively jettisoned the 'frantic dogma' of personal incorporeality – either tacitly to assume or even openly to assert that nomological propositions carry no entailments of physical necessity or physical impossibility. Thus Moritz Schlick, Convenor of the old original Vienna Circle, used to distinguish, rightly, descriptive from prescriptive laws, and then to assert, equally rightly, that laws of nature are descriptive not prescriptive (Schlick, [1931] 1939, ch. VII). Possibly following Schlick, it is then argued that 'the very word "determinism" is in some degree misleading. ... And the same applies to the use, in this context, of the word "necessity" and even of the word "cause" itself. ... But ... the fact is simply that when an event of one type occurs, an event of another type occurs also, in a certain temporal or spatio-temporal relation to the first. The rest is only metaphor' (Ayer, [1956] 1982, p. 22). As we shall be seeing ever more clearly, the truth is – and this is no metaphor – that nomological propositions do indeed describe; but that what they describe is not just ultimately coincidental regularities, but regularities which are practically necessary, and which it is therefore practically impossible to disrupt.

Edwards reminds us of how familiar we all are with such necessities and such impossibilities:

> All men find, and begin to find in early childhood, that there are innumerable things that can't be done, which they desire to do; and innumerable things which they are averse to, that must be, they can't avoid them, they will be whether they choose them or no. 'Tis to express this necessity, which men so soon and so often find, and which so greatly and so early affects them in innumerable cases, that such terms and phrases are first formed; and 'tis to signify such a necessity, that they are first used, and that they are most constantly used, in the common affairs of life ... ([1756] 1957, IV. 3, p. 352).

Edwards goes on at once to urge – surely with Hume's *Treatise* in his sights – that physical necessity must always be the primary notion: 'and not any such metaphysical, speculative and abstract notion, as that connection in the nature or course of things, which is between the subject and predicate of a proposition, and which is the foundation of the certain truth of that proposition.' Edwards, however, never succeeds in developing anything like a satisfactory account of the nature of logical necessity. Indeed, it is to this failure that we should put down almost all the intellectual weaknesses of his book. But he is very clear in his perception of the natures of and the differences between natural (physical) and moral necessity; and most emphatic in his consequent insistence that what was in his day called moral necessity is in truth no sort of necessity at all.

'It must be observed,' he concludes, 'that in what has been explained, as signified by . . . "moral necessity", . . . "necessity" is not used according to the original design and meaning of the word . . . ' (ibid., p. 159). For 'In the strictest propriety of speech, a man has a thing in his power if he has it in his choice, or at his election: and a man can't truly be said to be unable to do a thing, when he can do it if he will' (ibid., p. 162). All the examples which Edwards cites, both here and elsewhere, are, as they should be, cases in which a 'moral necessity' and a corresponding 'moral inability' or 'moral impossibility' is attributed to persons who, in the more profound sense, could do otherwise, if they chose: 'A woman of great honor and chastity may have a moral inability to prostitute herself to her slave. A child of great love and duty to his parents, may be unable to . . . kill his father. A very lascivious man . . . may be unable to forbear gratifying his lust', and so on (ibid., p. 160).

Before concluding this present section note needs to be taken of two common ways in which those seized of the truth that physical are radically different from moral causes are likely to go wrong. The first is by insisting that anyone saying that some event had not a physical but a moral cause is thereby implying that it occurred by chance. Thus, in a much reprinted article by one of the few contemporary philosophers whose name is known to a wider public, we read:

> Either it is an accident that I choose to act as I do or it is
> not. If it is an accident, then it is merely a matter of chance

that I did not choose otherwise; and if it is merely a matter of chance that I did not choose otherwise, it is surely irrational to hold me responsible for choosing as I did. But if it is not an accident that I choose to do one thing rather than another, then presumably there is some causal explanation of my choice: and in that case we are led back to determinism (Ayer, 1966, p. 18).

This argument, as shoddy and shameful as it has been popular, was dismissed most crisply two and a half centuries ago: 'The word "chance" always means something done without design. Chance and design stand in direct opposition to each other, and "chance" can never be properly applied to the acts of the will, which is the spring of all design, and which designs to choose whatsoever it does choose ... ' (Watts, [1723] 1811, VI, p. 268). I confess that this fine quotation is no trophy of my own reading of the six massive volumes of *The Works of the Reverend and Learned Isaac Watts D. D.* It is borrowed from Edwards ([1756] 1957, II. 13, p. 271), who himself seems a shade reluctant to take the point.

Here the most appropriate way to illustrate the second of these mistakes is by repeating the breathtaking sentences of a paragraph previously quoted by Vesey (p. 12): 'What distinguishes agent-causation from ordinary causation is that no expansion into a tale of two events is possible, and no law lurks. By the same token, nothing is explained' (Davidson, 1980, p. 53). So much for what, in deference to Max Weber, we call *verstehen* explanations. In so far as these are explanations in terms of moral rather than physical causes they are not, in Davidson's book, explanations at all.

In order to bring out just how wildly paradoxical and preposterous this is, let us look again at Skinner's *Beyond Freedom and Dignity*. Falsely believing that anthropomorphic and, in particular, teleological notions were expelled from physics not because they are not applicable to the inanimate but because they are essentially superstitious, Skinner becomes committed to arguing both that there can be no place for such concepts even in the sciences of man and, with Davidson, that explanations in these terms are not a genuine sort of explanation. Thus Skinner writes: 'If we ask someone, "Why did you go to the theatre", and he says, "Because I felt like going", we are apt to take his reply as a kind of explanation' (1973, pp. 12–13). We are indeed. For that 'I wanted to go to the theatre' may fully explain conduct previously puzzling. What of course these responses will not do is answer as well as set those further questions which Skinner and others may quite reasonably wish to press: why do I have a taste, and this particular taste, for the theatre, and so on.

But all this, of course, constitutes no sufficient reason to proclaim the illegitimacy of all explanation in terms of moral causes. Such imperialist proclamations on behalf of the physical sciences must appear yet more unwarranted and intolerant if and when we recall that *verstehen* explanations possess a kind of primacy over their present rivals: 'Perhaps the simplest and most psychologically satisfying explanation of any observed phenomenon is that it happened that way because someone wanted it to happen that way' (Sowell, 1980, p. 97).

# 4 Senses, and Nonsenses, of 'Necessity'

Already two very relevant and basic points about necessity have been made for us by Jonathan Edwards, with decisive force. First, and against Hume, Edwards urged that we all of us, from our earliest years, have had and continue to have experience of physical necessity. Next, and against all comers, he insisted that what was in his day called moral necessity is not in fact any kind of necessity at all.

Two things led Hume to deny physical necessity. First, there was his fundamental empiricist commitment. He wanted to show, and I believe succeeds in showing, that, for all anyone could know a priori, any thing or sort of thing might be the cause of any other thing or sort of thing. Indeed, we could not know a priori that everything, or anything, must have a cause. So Hume had to show that we can never discern any logical necessities somehow linking together different objects or sorts of objects in the non-linguistic world. Second, there was his Cartesian commitment to admit as experience only whatever might be accessible to some incorporeal subject, congenitally incapable of action; rather than what actually is available to flesh and blood human beings, both acting upon and being affected by a knowably material environment. (For defence of this interpretation compare Flew, 1986.)

The *Treatise* was very much a young man's book, one sometimes not unsympathetically described as Hume's *Language, Truth and Logic*. In his discussion there 'Of liberty and necessity' Hume denounces 'the doctrine of liberty' as 'fantastical': it is 'absurd . . . in one sense, and unintelligible in any other' ([1739] 1978, II.iii.1 and 2, pp. 407, 404 and 407). Both his reasons and his vehemence would commend him to Skinner. But in the first *Enquiry*, under exactly the same heading, Hume presents a 'reconciling project' with regard to 'the most contentious question of metaphysics, the most contentious science' ([1787] 1975, VIII.i, p. 95). Despite this striking difference of tone and temper the substance of both treatments is very similar.

In both Hume starts from the necessities or alleged necessities which, he contends, are both presupposed and discovered not only by the moral sciences but also in everyday life; although he does in both eventually go on to notice possible theological implications of conclusions about what is for him the primary problem. In both Hume sees his contribution as a corollary of findings from the investigation of causation: 'Our author pretends', as the *Abstract* has it, 'that this reasoning puts the whole controversy in a new light, by giving a new definition of "necessity" ' ([1740] 1978, p. 661: inverted commas supplied).

Proposed as that it is new indeed! Nevertheless, we cannot protest either too soon or too often that what Hume is offering is in truth not so much a fresh account of the meaning of the word 'necessity', as, rather, a denial that there is any such thing as that to which that word, as previously understood, pretended to refer. Persistent and reiterated protest is required. For Hume himself, here and elsewhere, constantly employs both that particular word and various semantic associates in senses far stronger than anything for which he is officially prepared to provide. Consider again, for instance, the passage from the *Treatise* quoted by Vesey (pp. 22–3).

When, however, Hume sets himself to demonstrate that human action is subject to the same inexorable necessity, what he in fact attempts, and considers that he succeeds in doing, is much more modest. It is to argue only that there are everywhere to be discovered universal and reliable regularities. Certainly his actual, more modest enterprise is well worth attempting. Far too many people have been inclined to argue that the human world is that of *Hellzapoppin'*: 'where anything may happen, and it probably will'. It is important to bring out that there are sufficient and sufficiently universal regularities in actual human behaviour for both moral science and social life to be possible; even if it has not been shown, and perhaps cannot be, that completely true, absolutely universal generalizations are everywhere to be found. As we shall see clearly when we come to contrast the intractable problems posed by claims to omnipotence with comparatively manageable difficulties arising from mere omniscience, there is an often crucial difference: between, on the one hand, maintaining that all future human behaviour is in principle predictable, because always causally necessitated; and, on the other hand, asserting only that there is and will continue to be sufficient regularity for knowledge of future human behaviour to be possible, notwithstanding that the behaviour of agents as such necessarily cannot be thus physically necessitated.

What in the *Treatise* Hume distinguishes as two senses of 'liberty' are 'the liberty of *spontaneity*, as it is call'd in the schools, and the liberty of *indifference*; . . . that which is oppos'd to violence, and that which means a negation of necessity and causes' ([1739] 1978, II.iii.2, p. 407). The reconciliation negotiated in the first *Enquiry* interprets liberty in the first of these two ways. Hume is thus following in the compatibilist tracks of Hobbes. In chapter XXI of his *Leviathan*, Hobbes wrote: '*Liberty*, or *freedom* signifieth, properly, the absence of opposition; by *opposition* I mean external impediments of motion . . . '. In this understanding, in order to effect a reconciliation, it is not even required that 'a new definition of necessity' be introduced. For, as Hume himself says, 'this hypothetical liberty is universally allowed to belong to everyone who is not a prisoner and in chains' ([1748] 1975, VIII.i, p. 95).

The need for that 'new definition' here is to meet the suggestion that we who are, happily, neither prisoners nor in chains nevertheless remain subject to the same total physical necessitation as the planets and the stars. For, as Hobbes had seen most clearly, an inanimate piece of mechanism may truly be said to be free to move in this way or that, notwithstanding that it may be fully determined by physical causes to move or not to move in one way and no other. The better to understand the issues here it will help to say more about that Scholastic distinction.

The 'liberty of spontaneity' was a matter of being unhindered from doing what one wants to do; including, be it noted, performing those uncongenial duties which, in another sense of 'want', we do not want to perform (Flew, 1975, 51–2). The 'liberty of indifference' was, surely, not traditionally defined as, though it surely does imply, at least in the physical senses of the words, 'a negation of necessity and causes'? The crux was, in what we have been calling the more profound sense, the ability to do otherwise. Thus the Spanish Jesuit Luis Molina spoke of this sort of liberty as involved when, 'given all necessary conditions for acting, it is within the agent's power to act or not to act' (quoted by Kenny, 1975, p. 123). This, so far as it goes, is a satisfactory explication. But what it explicates is not an everyday sense of 'liberty' so much as that ability to do otherwise which is essential not only to free agency but to agency as such.

Given these fuller understandings of the two expressions, 'the liberty of indifference' would appear to be presupposed by, rather than sharply separated from, 'the liberty of spontaneity'. Certainly if our previous account of desire is correct, and if desires do not necessitate the actions which they may motivate, then to explain behaviour in terms of the motives of the behavers must presuppose that they were in so behaving agents; who therefore could, in the more profound sense, have done other than they did. This observation parallels our earlier insistence that, in the interpretation of 'could no other' appropriate in the case of Luther before the Diet of Worms, that 'he could no other' presupposes that, in the more profound sense, he could. But it is altogether different with being free to move, in the way in which anyone or anything is free to move in as much as it is not by physical obstructions prevented from moving. Yet this is the only kind of freedom which Hume is here trying to reconcile with anything.

Most importantly, Hume's boasted 'reconciling project' makes no attempt at the impossible task of reconciling an all-embracing physical necessity with the powers of agents to do either this or that, at will. This insoluble problem can scarcely arise for Hume since he doubts the legitimacy of both ideas; and is quite certain that, even if legitimate, they have no application in the universe as it in fact is. His conclusion about the powers of agents he offers at the end of his account 'Of the idea of necessary connexion' in the *Treatise*, as a corollary: 'The distinction which we often make betwixt *power* and the *exercise* of it, is . . . without foundation' ([1739] 1978, I.iii.14, p. 171). All this makes it rather remarkable that section VIII of the first *Enquiry* has become a foundation document for compatibilists; including, I shamefacedly confess, myself when young.

Part of the explanation may lie in the fact that Hume does provide materials for a different, possible and necessary reconciliation: between, on the one hand, the subsistence of these by him unrecognized agent powers to do otherwise, and, on the other hand, the subsistence in human affairs of a great deal of regularity – miscalled by him necessity. This reconciliation is required if we are to have any rational prediction of human conduct; and if would-be moral scientists are to be saved from a ruinous commitment to deny those distinguishing truths about human nature both presupposed and cherished in 'the literature of dignity' (Skinner, 1973, p. 55). Happily it is also possible. For, as Hume so usefully reminds us, we are all of us all the time making such predictions, and relying on their correctness. If we could not do this, and if we were not pretty regularly right, then life in constant interaction with other people would become impossible. Perhaps moral scientists will become able, more often than the rest of us – perhaps some already have become able – to predict in what senses people confronted with the need will in fact choose. But this in itself will have no tendency to show that such choices will not really be choices, and that the chooser could not have chosen otherwise. For there is a world of difference between, on the one hand, knowing that someone will in fact act thus and thus, and on the other hand, knowing that they are willy nilly, necessitated so to behave.

This crucial difference is most elegantly displayed, in a theological context, by the Renaissance Humanist Lorenzo Valla (1405–57). (It was he who, as a Papal Secretary, first demonstrated that the *Donation of Constantine* is a forgery!) Valla's 'Dialogue on Free Will', mediated perhaps through Bayle or Leibniz, was very probably Hume's ultimate source for the suggestion that we are all apt here to be misled by what Popper has christened the 'Oedipus Effect'. This he defines as 'the influence of an item of information upon the situation to which the information refers' (Popper, 1957, p. 13; and compare Hume, [1748] 1975, p. 96).

The temptation here is to mistake as showing that foreknowledge of human conduct is impossible in principle, the possibility that someone will respond to being told what he or she will do by so acting as to falsify that prediction. What it does demonstrate is that intending predictors must take care: either that their predictions are not communicated to the subjects – or should it be the objects? – of those predictions; or else that they have themselves taken due account of the subjects' – or objects' – possible responses to such communications. The elegance of Valla's delightful dialogue, which deserves a place on the preparatory reading list of anyone aspiring to contribute to our present discussion, is seen best in his employment of a typically Humanist device:

> . . . although the wisdom of God cannot be separated from His power and will, I may by this device of Jupiter and Apollo separate them. What cannot be achieved with one god may be achieved with two, each having his own proper nature – the one for creating the character of men, the other for knowing – that it may appear that foreknowledge is not the cause of necessity but that all this, whatever it is,

must be referred to the will of God (Valla [1405–57] 1968, p. 174).

Failures to appreciate the different natures of logical and physical necessity, or correctly and systematically to distinguish their different locations, have given rise to a vast amount of confusion in the present context. The best way to sort this out is to work on The Problem of the Seafight, which first appears in the literature in chapter IX of Aristotle's *de Interpretatione*. (From the tautological truth that there either will or will not be a seafight tomorrow, it is alleged to follow that whatever will in fact occur will occur necessarily and unavoidably.) The fact that so many able, even great, philosophers and theologians have in the past made such heavy weather of these problems shows how hard it must have been to master for the first time basics which may now seem entirely obvious. It is not so easy either to explain or to excuse the failure on the part of some contemporary philosophers, enjoying the advantage of training in more modern schools, to apply these basics to the issues raised by that ancient problem.

In Aristotle it was presented as an argument, which he himself rejected, for fatalism; fatalism being the doctrine that what is going to happen is fated to happen, in the sense that it will happen inevitably and regardless of what anyone does or tries to do in order to stop it happening. In more recent times, this argument, known to Gottfried Leibniz (1646–1715) and his contemporaries as 'The Lazy Sophism', became popular with the song sung by Miss Doris Day in one of her films, 'Che sarà, sarà. Whatever will be, will be'.

It should be immediately obvious that any such argument must be fallacious. For, in so far as it is an argument and not merely the reiterated assertion of a commended conclusion, it proceeds from a premise which is tautological, and hence a necessary truth of logic. Spelt out in a helpfully illuminating symbolism, this premise amounts to no more than the uncontentious truism that, for all values of x, from *x will happen* it follows necessarily that *x will happen*. From such an only too true premise no substantial or contentious conclusion could be validly deduced. For the conclusions of valid deductive arguments are always contained in their premises; in the sense that such arguments are defined as those in which you cannot assert the premise or premises while denying the conclusion without thereby contradicting yourself. Once all this is appreciated, and given that spelling out in the helpfully illuminating symbolism, it becomes easy to pick out the nerve of the fallacy. (If anyone were to intervene here to protest that a merely notational innovation cannot really matter, the best first reply is to offer them some exercises: perhaps starting with a few calculations to be done in Roman not Arabic numerals; and then continuing with the development of a chemical argument purely in words, and without benefit of the now standard symbolism invented by the Baron Berzelius.)

That nerve lies in a tricky quickstep: first we uproot the adverb 'necessarily' from its original and proper position modifying the verb 'follows'; then we intrude it into the conclusion so that that now becomes, without any legitimizing warrant, the quite different *x will necessarily happen*; and finally we interpret that adverb, as the context of its fresh placing makes most appropriate, to refer not to logical but to physical necessity.

Much has already been done to elucidate the nature and locus of physical necessity and physical impossibility. We now have to perform a similar exercise on logical necessity and logical impossibility. As Hume incompletely and somewhat dimly saw, logical necessities and logical impossibilities belong not in the physical world but in the universe of discourse. The complementary definitions of both notions refer to self-contradiction. It is, therefore, as wrong as it has often been found tempting to think of logical impossibility as somehow the limiting case upon a scale which finds physical impossibility somewhere around the halfway mark. The wrong idea is that what is physically impossible is impossible only for mortals, whereas the logically impossible transcends the resources even of omnipotence.

The truth is that a suggestion is said to involve a logical impossibility if that suggestion contains or implies a self-contradiction, or perhaps is in some other way incoherent and strictly unintelligible; whereas we speak of a logical necessity where it is the denial of the suggestion which involves or implies the self-contradiction. Thus it is a matter of logical necessity that, for all values of x, *x will be* entails *x will be*. By contrast, backwards causation is impossible logically. For it would require the possibility of either making something to have (already) happened which had not (already) happened, or else that of making something not to have happened notwithstanding that it in fact had (already) happened. As St Thomas Aquinas (c. 1225–76) puts the matter in the *Summa Theologica*, with his customary terse correctness: 'Whatever does not imply a contradiction is, consequently, among those possibilities in virtue of which God is described as omnipotent. But what does imply a contradiction is not subsumed under the divine omnipotence . . . ' (1926, I. Q25, A3). You cannot, he might still better have said, transmute some incoherent mixture of words into sense merely by introducing the three-letter word 'God' to be its grammatical subject.

Those who were in need of the pemmican elucidations of our previous paragraph should perhaps now test their burgeoning skills on the Hobbist variant of The Lazy Sophism. Hobbes took the argument to be valid, a proof not of fatalism but of a kind of determinism 'that all events have necessary causes' (1839–45, IV, p. 276). His version is found in a pamphlet 'Of Liberty and Necessity'. (The subtitle is, incidentally, too good to miss even though it was apparently not written by Hobbes but added by his piratical publisher: 'A treatise wherein all controversy concerning predestination, election, freewill, grace, merits, reprobation, etc. is fully decided and cleared.') For

Hobbes, being British, the weather was a topic of constant interest. So he writes: 'It is necessary that tomorrow it shall rain or not rain. If therefore it be not necessary that it shall rain, it is necessary that it shall not rain; otherwise there is no necessity that the proposition, *It shall rain or not rain*, should be true. I know there be some that say it may necessarily be true that one of the two shall come to pass, but not, singly, that it shall rain, or that it shall not rain. Which is as much as to say one of them is necessary, yet neither of them is necessary' (IV, p. 277).

The discussion is often complicated by the introduction of two further, equally fundamental notions: truth and knowledge. The additional arguments requiring these notions are: first, that, if it is true that *x will be*, then there must already be some unalterable corresponding fact for that proposition to be now truly stating; and, second, that, if there is to be knowledge of what is going to happen, then that present knowledge must have some present and – for the knowledge to be truly certain – now altogether unalterable object. This is called 'The Problem of Future Contingents', the problem being whether there are or could be true propositions about the future, propositions logically contingent as opposed to logically necessary. (A contingent proposition is, by definition, one of which the contradictory is not self-contradictory.) Since the truths of logic are timeless, not truths about happenings at particular times, there neither is nor could be any parallel 'Problem of Future Necessaries'.

Several of the greatest in philosophy – from Aristotle himself, on through William of Ockham (c. 1285–1349), and beyond – were tormented by this problem, often becoming in consequence tied up in paradoxical knots. Yet, once someone else has seen further, we can, having learnt to stand on their shoulders, pick out the route towards a satisfactory resolution. The main source of trouble, additional to those dealt with already, is a false model of empirical knowledge and, consequently, of empirical truth. This false model is found first in Plato's

*Republic*, in his account of a hierarchy of cognitive faculties (509dff.). Cognition is there construed on the model of perception. As sight, smell and hearing have their corresponding objects in sights, smells and sounds; so knowledge, belief and opinion all have to have their corresponding, but different, sorts of objects.

A second consequence follows, although this is not one which Plato himself drew out. For from *Jack can now see, or otherwise perceive, x* it follows that *x is now available to be, and being, seen, or otherwise perceived*. So anyone employing the perceptual model is bound to infer that any knowledge of temporal facts can only be of events occurring simultaneously with that knowing. (It is by employing this false model, and by making a sound inference therefrom, that many philosophers of parapsychology have been misled to argue that the occurrence of paranormal precognition would show that, somehow, the future is already here. See, for instance, the article 'Precognition' in Edwards (1967).

Were the perceptual model correct, however, we should also have to infer that there can be no knowledge, just as there can indeed be no perception, of anything presently outwith the range of our senses. So, unless we are prepared to cherish this preposterous conclusion, we have to abandon that model. This leaves us with no warrant whatever for insisting, contrary to all familiar practice and experience, that present knowledge can only be of present facts.

In so far as empirical truth is construed as involving always some sort of correspondence between true proposition and whatever that true proposition asserts to be the case, it becomes similarly tempting, yet for similar reasons equally wrong, to insist that such correspondence can only be with unalterably present facts.

The further point to grasp about truth is that the 'is' of 'It is true that *x will happen*' is, or should be, timeless. Ideally, all temporal reference ought to be built into the propositions themselves. These would then become timelessly true; or, as the case might be, timelessly false. Certainly, what Immanuel Kant (1724–1804) so loved to call apodeictic words or expressions – words or expressions such as (logically) 'necessary' and (logically) 'impossible' – belong in statements of the logical relations between propositions. But the dates on which events have happened, are happening, or will happen belong inside, and are essential elements in, specific assertions of their occurrence.

Of course, it is and will remain perfectly correct and idiomatic English to utter such sentences as 'It would no longer be true now to say that the Labour Party is staunchly anti-totalitarian and wholeheartedly pro-NATO'. Yet philosophers, and even plain persons while doing philosophy, need to be on guard. For long experience has shown that by such idioms we may be misled to think that one and the same proposition may at different times be both true and false. Or to believe that, if propositions about future human behaviour could be both true and known to be true, then it could not also be both true and known to be true that the behavers will (sometimes) be agents; and so able, in the profounder sense, to do other than they will do.

# 5 The Compatibilism of Faith

I turn now to the problems of agency and necessity as these arise for those considering the claims of Mosaic theism; the theism, that is, which is common to Judaism, Christianity and Islam. The previous section has, surely, shown that there is no necessary incompatibility between, first, the assertion that God always knows what all human agents will in fact do; and, second, the contentions that our actions are indeed ours, that they could have been other than they were, and that they can in consequence properly be held to our individual accounts. If there is any incompatibility here it has to be, as Valla argued, between, on the one hand (not God's omniscience but) God's omnipotence, and, on the other hand (all or some of) that second cluster of complementary contentions. In order, with Milton, 'to justify the ways of God to man' the theist philosopher theologian must obviously be a compatibilist – even if to achieve this he has, with Luther, to resort to a faith which defies all reason.

It was, therefore, as I remarked in section 1, both obtuse and ignorant to define 'predestination' as involving only foreknowledge. Quite apart from the objection taken by those theists who maintain that the God who works in and through human history is nevertheless himself somehow 'outside time', and hence that it must be incorrect to attribute either foreknowledge or hindsight to that God, such a definition is deist rather than theist in its suggestion that, after the God of Moses created the universe 'in the beginning', he left it alone, to run on – even if always strictly according to plan – independently. What crucially distinguishes Mosaic theism from deism is the theists' claim that their God not only created the universe 'in the beginning', but also remains always the ultimate sustaining cause of all creation. In the words of William Temple, Archbishop of Canterbury during the 1940s, without that constant support everything and everyone 'would collapse into non-existence'. Or, as Mahalia Jackson sings it, 'He's got the whole world in his hands'.

Once this message is taken fully and deeply to head it should become obvious that the usual imagery is utterly inappropriate. It is indeed egregiously inept, as is so persistently done, to compare the relation of Creator to creatures with the relation of a great Father to his often prodigal sons, and sometimes delinquent daughters. For, especially once they are grown up, a father can direct the behaviour of his children only through the presentation to them of what they themselves choose to construe as reasons for acting in the senses directed. To bring out the constant, total, yet largely unwitting dependence of creature upon Creator no mundane analogy can, in the nature of the case, be altogether adequate. Perhaps the least wretched is that of a Great Manipulator/Hypnotist, whose un-recognized yet irresistible post-hypnotic suggestions his subjects cannot but fulfil.

Consider, for example, two passages in the *Summa contra Gentiles* ([c. 1225–74] 1955) where Aquinas points these immediate implications of theism in lucid and pedestrian prose:

> ... just as God not only gave being to things when they first began, but is also – as the conserving cause of being – the cause of their being as long as they last ... so he also not only gave things their operative powers when they were first created, but is also always the cause of these in things. Hence, if this divine influence stopped every operation would stop. Every operation, therefore, of anything is traced back to him as its cause (III, p. 67).

This is spelt out more fully in two later chapters:

> God alone can move the will, as an agent, without doing violence to it. ... Some people ... not understanding how God can cause a movement of our will in us without

prejudicing the freedom of the will, have tried to explain
. . . authoritative texts wrongly: that is, they would say
that God 'works in us, to wish and to accomplish' means
that he causes in us the power of willing, but not in such a
way that he makes us will this or that. . . . These people
are, of course, opposed quite plainly by authoritative texts
of Holy Writ. For it says in *Isaiah* (xxvi, 2), 'Lord, you
have worked all our work in us'. Hence we receive from
God not only the power of willing but its employment also
(III, pp. 88–9).

Lest anyone should protest that the revelation of the
*New Testament* is in this matter milder, consider too the
passage in which St Paul expatiates upon the same
prophetic theme. In *Romans* (9:18–23) we read:

Therefore hath he mercy upon whom he will have mercy,
and whom he will be hardeneth. Thou wilt say then unto
me, 'Why doth he yet find fault? For who hath resisted his
will?' Nay but, O man, who are thou that repliest against
God? Shall the thing formed say to him that formed it,
'Why has thou made me thus?' Hath not the potter power
over the clay, of the same lump to make one vessel unto
honour, and another unto dishonour? What if God, willing
to shew his wrath, and to make his power known, endured
with much longsuffering the vessels of wrath fitted to
destruction; and that he might make known the riches of
his glory on the vessels of mercy, which he had afore
prepared unto glory? (Compare, for further biblical references, Edwards, [1756] 1957, *passim*.)

A remarkably restrained comment of Einstein's is typical
both of his humane sympathies and of his radical
directness of mind. Einstein was certainly, in the Mosaic
understanding, an atheist. That he once asserted, in
response to a telegraphic query, that he believed in
Spinoza's God, should deceive nobody. For Spinoza himself
spoke always of 'God or Nature', as equivalent. So too
when Einstein affirmed that 'The Lord God does not play
dice!' he was not defending the God of Abraham, Isaac

and Israel against a gambling rap, but protesting the world picture presented by quantum mechanics. His actual assessment of theism was this:

> Nobody, certainly, will deny that the idea of the existence of an omnipotent, just, and omnibeneficent personal God is able to accord man solace, help, and guidance. . . . But, on the other hand, there are decisive weaknesses attached to this idea in itself, which have been painfully felt since the beginning . . . if this being is omnipotent then every occurrence, including every human action, every human thought, and every human feeling and aspiration, is also his work. How is it possible to think of holding men responsible for their deeds and thoughts before such an almighty Being? In giving out punishments and rewards he would be . . . passing judgement on himself (Einstein, 1950, pp. 26–7).

It has often been thought, and said, even by those paid to know better, and to teach what they know, that the horrific harshness of predestinationism – with its inescapable implication that God makes people do what he proposes later to damn them for having done – is some sort of eccentricity peculiar and confined to Calvinist ultras. This is quite wrong. In fact, among the intellectually first class the differences are in the force and frankness of expression rather than in substantial doctrine. How could it be otherwise, once the theist doctrine of creation as constant and total dependence is taken seriously?

Calvin was, of course, as almost everyone knows, uninhibited in insisting that God must be the ultimate author of human sin, as of everything else: 'The ears of some are offended when one says that God willed it. But I ask you, what else is the permission of him who is entitled to forbid, or rather who has the thing in his own hands, but an act of will?' (quoted Leibniz, [1710] 1951, p. 222: I refer here to a secondary authority because it is itself a classic; and a rich compendium of both clear statements of, and frantic attempts to avoid, this Calvinist consequence).

But you can find substantially the same thing in many other, perhaps more surprising sources. Perhaps most surprising, at any rate to those aware of the present condition of that organization, is the 1922 Commission report on *Doctrine in the Church of England*. This admitted 'that the whole course of events is under the control of God . . . logically this involves the affirmation that there is no event, and no aspect of any event, even those due to sin and so contrary to the Divine will, which falls outside the scope of his purposive activity' (p. 47).

Again, the *Summa Theologica* contains a Question 'Of Predestination' in which the Angelic Doctor himself lays it down: 'As men are ordained to eternal life through the providence of God, it likewise is part of that providence to permit some to fall away from that end; this is called reprobation. . . . Reprobation implies not only foreknowledge but also something more'. Aquinas shrinks from saying that God is the cause of sin, notwithstanding that his premises require this conclusion. But he has to allow that although reprobation 'is not the cause of what is in the present — namely, sin; nevertheless it is the cause of abandonment by God. It is the cause . . . of what is assigned in the future — namely, eternal punishment' (I.xxiii.3).

If this is, as of course it is, the best which even the Angelic Doctor can do in rational defence of the compatibilist conclusion that a Creator may justly hold his creatures accountable for what he makes them do, then it is time to turn to the alternative preferred by Martin Luther (1483–1546). Noticing that Luther wrote *de Servo Arbitrio* and St Augustine *de Libero Arbitrio*, but then forgetting that Luther was an Augustinian friar, some have falsely assumed that their doctrines were as contrary as the titles of these books. We begin to suspect the truth that this is false when we find the Reformer saying: 'Now, by "necessarily" I do not mean "compulsorily" . . . a man without the Spirit of God does not do evil against his will, under pressure, as though he were taken by the scruff of his neck and dragged into it, like a thief or a footpad being dragged off against his will to punishment; but he does it spontaneously and voluntarily' ([1525] 1969, p. 139).

Certainly not compulsorily; for the necessity which Luther meant was that imposed by the Creator's total and constantly exercised manipulative power. Yet to reconcile that with individual human responsibilities must indeed exceed all the capacities of reason. So Luther points an alternative:

> The highest degree of faith is to believe He is just, though of His own will he makes us ... proper subjects for damnation, and seems (in the words of Erasmus) 'to delight in the torments of poor wretches and to be a fitter object for hate than for love'. If I could by any means understand how this same God ... can yet be merciful and just, there would be no need for faith (ibid., p. 138: and compare and contrast Hume, [1748] 1975, VIII.ii and Schopenhauer, [1841] 1960, IV).

Later Luther addresses himself to the question: 'Why then does He not alter those evil wills which He moves?' Understandably, if unsatisfactorily, Erasmus receives no answer here:

> It is not for us to inquire into these mysteries, but to adore them. If flesh and blood take offence here and grumble, well, let them grumble; they will achieve nothing; grumbling will not change God! And however many of the ungodly stumble and depart, the elect will remain (ibid., p. 137).

But the Reformer, unlike the author of the *Summa Theologica*, was not so completely the complacent appar-atchik as to proceed to a cool summary of the reasons why – very properly – 'the blessed in glory will have no pity for the damned' (III.Supp.xciv. 1–3). Or as we used to say in the unhallowed ranks of the Royal Air Force, 'Damn you, Jack, I'm fireproof!'

## 6 Back to Godfrey Vesey

Section 5 of my contribution has presented in its most ferocious form an antimony far more intractable than that with which Vesey first left us, in hopes of thereby providing him with a serviceable cue to tell us what he now wants to say about agency and physical determinism. In order further to ease the return from religious nightmares to secular science, I simply highlight what to some may seem a crucial difference between predestinationism and a correspondingly universal, necessitating, atheist, physical determinism. Whereas in the former responsibility must at the very least be shared with, if not shifted wholly on to, the supposed Great Manipulator, in the latter there is and can be no one else to blame. As that most characteristic desk motto of President Harry S. Truman had it: 'The buck stops here!'.

# Hume's Compatibilism

GODFREY VESEY

# 1    Recapitulation and Reaction

I began my first contribution by saying that the issue to be debated by Antony Flew and myself is that of agency and necessity: human agency and causal necessity. It is not a purely academic issue; it has practical implications, as is shown by the fact that psychologists, such as B. F. Skinner, who want to put their psychological knowledge to use in changing men's behaviour for the better, feel it necessary to discredit the notion that human behaviour is attributable to 'an autonomous controlling agent'. This notion, Skinner thinks, is pre-scientific. A scientist attributes behaviour to the environment: 'an experimental analysis shifts the determination of behaviour from autonomous man to the environment — an environment responsible both for the evolution of the species and for the repertoire acquired by each member'.

Skinner ascribes the notion he wants to discredit to the early Greeks. He is right to do so. Plato distinguished between two kinds of causes: in brief, 'mind' and 'necessity'; more fully, things 'which are endowed with mind and are the workers of things fair and good' and 'things which, being moved by others, are compelled to move others'. The former (things endowed with mind) correspond to what Skinner calls 'autonomous controlling agents'.

Whether it is pre-scientific or not, the notion that we are agents certainly reflects something in our everyday talk. We say, for example, 'Socrates sat down', thereby distinguishing the situation from one in which his legs simply gave way, and he found himself in a sitting position whether he liked it or not. Sitting involves movements of muscles, bones in their joints, and so on. Plato raises the question of how what Socrates does relates to what is physically necessary for his legs to bend. Expressed in terminology that found favour in the 1960s, this is the question of how 'agent causation' related to 'event causation'.

Socrates says: 'Since the bones move freely in their joints, the sinews by relaxing and contracting enable me somehow to bend my limbs'. Somehow, but how? His sinews relax and contract; does *he* relax and contract them? If not, does he do something else – send a message down a nerve, or perform an act of will – that makes them relax and contract?

A 'thought experiment' to help us with this question is provided by the case of William James' patient who is astonished to find that a movement he was asked to make had not taken place. Did he do anything to make him think he had raised his hand? Aristotle's uncompromising answer, I said, would be: 'No. It seemed to him as if he raised his hand (apart from not feeling it rise) but in fact he did not do anything'. Descartes' answer (and James' answer, too: see James, 1891, vol. II, p. 560) would be: 'Yes. He willed his hand to rise'. A third possible answer is: 'Yes. He tried to raise his hand'. Anticipating (wrongly, as it transpired) that Flew would prefer this third answer, I discussed it at some length, aligning myself with O'Shaughnessy on the question of how trying is related to doing: that is, 'internally' and not as a Humian case.

Whether Descartes thought of an act of will as an external cause is questionable. What he said about 'the union between body and soul' might be taken as a way of saying that the relationship between willing and doing is internal. But this is not the standard interpretation. In terms of the agent causation/event causation distinction, what Descartes did, according to the standard interpretation, was to put an event causation construction on a fact of agent causation.

Once a voluntary movement is treated, not as caused immediately by the agent, but as caused by something else, the way is open for a further causal question, about the 'something else'. And if the answer is thought to allow of yet another causal question ('What causes people to will as they do?') then we are well and truly launched on the slippery slope at the bottom of which is the rejection of any autonomous agency whatsoever, any personal responsibility for human behaviour. We are on the way to joining Skinner and company, though to get to Skinner we have to revise our conception of psychology. We have to abjure the introspectionism of Hume, the Mills, Bain and Titchener, and to recant its enabling doctrine, that of the association of ideas. We have to embrace, instead, the behaviourism of Watson, Thorndike and Skinner, and to adopt the paradoxical faith that what Skinner calls 'operant conditioning' is like Pavlovian conditioning in leaving no room for autonomous agency. I call it a 'paradoxical faith' because operant conditioning differs from Pavlovian conditioning precisely in being dependent on there being something the experimental subject does of its, his, or her own accord, such as pulling a piece of string. It is, in short, dependent on an exercise of agency. Without the agent (non-human or human) *doing something* (in the sense of 'doing something' in which a reflex response, such as salivation, is *not* doing something) there would be no behaviour to be 'reinforced' by 'conditioning'. I concluded from this that the actual facts of instrumental learning do not warrant B. F. Skinner's charge against the early Greeks that they committed a 'fatal flaw' in attributing human behaviour to autonomous agents.

There remains, however, a more intractable question. Agent causation is characterized by the agent's being at liberty to move or not. But is it not true that all movements can be brought under a deterministic system of physical laws; that is, that it is physically determined that such-and-such movements will, or will not, take place? If so, does it not follow that there is really no such thing as agent causation?

At this point I handed over to Antony Flew. He began by saying that he could see no possibility of really substantial disagreement with me, save perhaps with regard to the more intractable question, the one about physical determinism. He approves of my starting out from Skinner, who wants to remove autonomous controlling agents from the scene in order to leave it free for psychologists, using their knowledge of how the environment works on people, to do the controlling (in what they conceive to be man's best interests, of course). Flew has evidently been a Skinner-watcher for longer than I have: he quotes relevant anti-free-will passages from Skinner's earlier works.

Flew distinguishes, as I did not, between Plato and Aristotle as 'the Founding Fathers of two rival traditions about the nature of man' – crudely, dualism (Plato) and monism (Aristotle) about body and mind. One reservation I have about this relates to his use of the expression 'Platonic–Cartesian' for the body–mind dualist position. I take the metaphysical basis of Plato's dualism to be a distinction between the visible, as that in which opposites are confounded, and the intelligible, as that in which they are not (Plato, *Republic* VII. 524c), and the metaphysical basis of Descartes' dualism to be a distinction between extension (physical extension being assumed to be the same as geometrical extension), on the one hand, and thought or consciousness, on the other, as the essences of two different substances. The difference between these metaphysical bases for body–mind dualism seems to me to be so great as to make the expression 'Platonic–Cartesian' possibly misleading. What Flew is right about, of course, is that both Plato and Descartes clearly conceived of the possibility of the mind existing apart from the body. Another reservation I have is about Aristotle *not* conceiving of this possibility. In *De Anima*, Book III, Chapter 5, Aristotle says that there is one sense in which mind is what it is 'by virtue of becoming all things' and another sense in which it is what it is 'by virtue of making all things' (430a15). Aristotle holds that mind as 'becoming all things' is united with body and is destructible. But mind as 'making all things', he says, is immortal and eternal. I find these sayings very difficult to understand, and so cannot confidently assert that Aristotle did not hold any form of mind–body dualism.

Flew proceeds to deal with some popular misconceptions, such as the misconception that 'predestinarianism' is a doctrine about precognition when really it is a doctrine about preordination. He approves of people who write on agency and necessity having done their homework; that is, having examined the 'arguments, distinctions and objections which were urged, made, or put by the great men of old'. Doing so is a way of avoiding misconceptions. He thinks that one position especially deserving of examination is what he calls 'compatibilism' (a position about which I did not say anything in my opening contribution).

In his section 2 ('Physical and Moral Causes: Getting the Distinction Right'), Flew objects to talk of 'agent causation and event causation' on the ground that it 'is bound to suggest that the distinction is between different sorts of causing rather than between different senses of (the word) "cause" '. I think I see the point of the distinction between 'sorts' and 'senses'. But Flew goes on to make what seems to me to be a different point when he says that *the right distinction* is between the sense in which an agent is said *to be caused* to act (by being afforded a motive) and the sense in which anything else is said *to be caused* to occur. I agree that this is a valid distinction. But what does he mean by saying that it is 'the right distinction'? Does he mean that it is somehow more basic than the agent cause/event cause distinction? If so, I think he is wrong. Suppose someone, as is his wont, lights up a cigarette after a meal. He is the cause of the cigarette's being lit, but has he necessarily a motive for lighting it? Having a motive is a characteristic, but not even an invariable characteristic, of being an agent cause. It seems to me that the agent causation/event causation distinction is the more basic. Similarly, I think that Hume's distinction between moral causes ('all circumstances which are fitted to work on the minds as motives or reasons') and physical causes is a valid distinction, but I do not think it is the same as Plato's distinction between things 'endowed with mind' (gods and human beings) and 'things which, being moved by others, are compelled to move others'. Plato's distinction is more basic.

However, I think this disagreement between Flew and me is a disagreement about where the emphasis should be put, rather than a 'really substantial disagreement'. He wants the emphasis put on the sense in which an agent is said to be caused to act (by being afforded a motive) because he wants to insist on the distinction between moral determinism ('all actions may be explained in terms of . . . the agents' motives, purposes, intentions, and the like') and physical determinism. His point is that only determinism of the physical kind involves necessitation, and so presents a threat to freedom. I agree with Flew on the point that matters: what he calls 'moral determinism' does *not* involve necessitation, but physical determinism *does*. Compared to this point, the point that people often act without any thought of ends to be achieved is not very important. True, but not very important. (I grant, of course, that it can be made untrue by stipulating that pleasure is always a desired end; but I would remark that this stipulation seems a bit forced when one reflects that people carry on smoking despite realizing the consequences.)

In section 3 (Physical and Moral Causes: Profiting from the Distinction'), Flew gives examples (Priestley, Galton, Freud, Edwards) of people who assimilate the operation of moral causes to that of physical ones; that is, people who think of motives etc. as necessitating. He approves of my quotation from Tucker, to the contrary. He remarks on how the use of the popular pseudotechnical term 'drives' carries the strong unwarranted suggestion of being passively driven. Incidentally, Tucker says something similar about the term 'motive': he says we commonly style the final cause (e.g. health) of an action (e.g. walking) the 'motive' 'by a metaphor taken from mechanical engines which cannot play without some spring or other mover to set them at work' (Brown, 1970, p. 103).

It is obvious how we acquire the idea of a moral cause:

from having motives for our actions. But how do we acquire the idea of a physical cause, involving, as it does, the idea of necessitation? In the last part of his section 3 and the beginning of section 4 ('Senses, and Nonsenses, of "Necessity" ') Flew says quite a lot about Hume's treatment of this question. To comment adequately on this I would need, first, to set out my own understanding of Hume's position (see below).

Later in his section 4 Flew discusses 'the different natures of logical and physical necessity'. He thinks the best way to sort out the differences is to work on The Problem of the Seafight (Aristotle, *de Interpretatione*, ch. IX), and accordingly does so. I do not think there is ground for 'substantial disagreement' between us on this.

Flew's fifth section is entitled 'The Compatibilism of Faith', and is about the possibility, or, rather, the impossibility, of reconciling our actions' being preordained (not just preknown, but preordained) by God, and their being indeed ours, that is, properly to be held to our individual accounts. Flew feels strongly about this. He writes of 'the horrific harshness of predestinationism – with its inescapable implication that God makes people do what he proposes later to damn them for having done', and says that it is quite wrong to suppose that predestinationism is 'some sort of eccentricity peculiar and confined to Calvinist ultras'.

Flew is not alone in feeling strongly about predestinationism. As a child, when my father preached a sermon I had heard before, I used to read the 39 Articles of Religion at the end of the *Book of Common Prayer*. I wondered if I could ever bring myself to assent to them. The one I always came back to was Article 17, 'Of Predestination and Election'. I had several questions, of different kinds. Am I one of the Elect, one of those who can 'feel in themselves the working of the Spirit of Christ, mortifying the works of the flesh, and their earthly members, and drawing up their mind to high and heavenly things' or am I a 'curious and carnal person', predestined for damnation? What is the point of trying to believe, to have faith, to be good and loving, and so on, if it is decreed in advance who is to be delivered from curse and damnation and who is not? Why did God create people only to curse and damn them?

About ten years after I decided not to seek ordination (as a result of God preordaining that I should so decide?) I read section 41 of Descartes' *Principles of Philosophy*, Part 1, the section entitled 'How to reconcile the freedom of our will with divine preordination' (Descartes, [1644] 1985, vol. I, p. 206). I do not think the content of the section lives up to the title, and I cannot think of anything that would do so. Once again, Flew and I are in agreement.

In his final remarks Flew expresses the hope that what he has said about predestinationism will provide me with 'serviceable cue' to tell him, and the reader, what I have to say about agency and physical determinism. I do not think I can use it directly as a cue. I can, however, say something about the notion that an omnipotent God is the true cause of everything. I can do this if I approach the question of agency and physical determinism via a critical analysis of Hume's 'reconciling project'. Who knows, I may manage to provoke that longed-for 'really substantial disagreement', so that purchasers of this volume may feel they are getting their money's worth! Flew has written a lot on Hume, but I think there are some things I can say that he has not said, and they may well be things to which he will take exception.

# 2 Hume's Equipment

Anyone who takes on a job in philosophy, such as that of showing liberty and necessity to be compatible, does not come to it empty-minded. He comes to the job equipped with premises, definitions, principles, practices. He may not even be able to say what some of them are, they are so much a part of his whole outlook and approach. Then it is the task of his critic in a later century to make explicit what is implicit, and to evaluate the assumptions in the light of a new perspective.

What is Hume's equipment?

(1) One piece of it is clearly on view, and is, as clearly, false. Hume says that all mankind have always 'without hesitation acknowledged the doctrine of necessity in their whole practice and reasoning' (Hume, [1748] 1975, p. 95). They have not. The early Greeks made a point of contrasting necessity with something else: Plato, with mind (*Timaeus* 46c–48c, *Phaedo* 97c–99b), Aristotle, with things happening 'for the sake of something' (*Physics* 198b17). Only if 'all mankind' is restricted to the new scientists and their philosopher fellow-travellers does Hume's bold assertion seem at all plausible.

(2) Another piece of Hume's equipment that is clearly on view concerns motives. He writes of motives as 'passions' which 'produce actions, the same motive always producing the same action' (Hume, [1748] 1975, p. 83). 'The conjunction between motives and voluntary actions', he says, 'is as regular and uniform as that between the cause and effect in any part of nature' (ibid., p. 88). Hume evidently wants his reader to think of a motive as a mental event that is regularly followed by a particular action in much the same way as the physical event of one billiard ball striking another is regularly followed by a particular event, i.e. the second ball moving. In both cases there is a

constant conjunction of two objects, in a wide sense of 'object'. I will not repeat that both of us have said in our first contributions about motives as explanations of actions.

(3) Another piece of Hume's equipment that is on view is his definition of 'liberty'. Liberty is an agent's having 'a power of acting, or not acting, according to the determinations of the will' (ibid., p. 95). But it can hardly be said to be *clearly* on view, for the ambiguity of the second part of it needs to be pointed out to be seen. 'According to the determinations of the will' may mean either 'according to how *the will determines*' or 'according to how *the will is determined*'. Descartes could agree with the first interpretation, but not with the latter, for he held the will to be *undetermined*, free. Hume, on the other hand, sought acceptance of the definition with the second interpretation in mind; he wanted his readers to be persuaded that *the will is determined* – by motives. Descartes had played into Hume's hands by inventing 'acts of will'. Without any thought of 'the will' as a distinct mental faculty we would have been content with the unexceptionable first part of the definition: liberty consists in having a power of acting or not acting.

It is easy to think of examples to illustrate the first part of the definition. Take the case of a bright light being shone into your eyes, as happens at night when an approaching car driver has neglected to dip his headlights and you are subjected to his main beam. You are at liberty to close your eyes, or keep them open and direct your gaze away from his headlights. If you keep them open, you are *not* at liberty to narrow, or not narrow, the pupils of your eyes. That is a reflex response over which you have no control. You have a power of acting or not acting with respect to your eyes being open or closed; you have no such power with respect to the size of the pupils of your eyes.

It is not unreasonable to interpret Descartes as saying that you do *not* have a power of acting or not acting with respect to your eyes being open or closed; you only have a power of *willing or not willing* your eyes to be open or closed. Once this is said, there is the possibility of asking, say, 'How do you make your will operate to the effect that your eyes stay open?', and the possibility of answering, 'By letting the motive of keeping control of your car (for which you need to keep your eyes open), have more power over your will than the motive of protecting your eyes from glare'. If it is then asked 'And how do you do that?', there is the possibility of answering, 'It isn't something you do; it is just that your instinct for survival is more powerful than your momentary wish to protect your eyes from glare'. If it is then asked 'And why do you have this all-powerful instinct for survival?', there is the possibility of answering, 'Because the environment is such that only people who have such an instinct in fact survive, to produce offspring who are like them in having it'. And somewhere along this line the notion of a person, an autonomous agent, doing something, has foundered without trace. Event causation has taken over from agent causation. Descartes, by inventing acts of the will, made the takeover possible, but resisted it by declaring the will to be undetermined, free. Hume, by defining 'liberty' in terms of 'the determinations of the will', helped the takeover on its way.

(4) A fourth piece of Hume's equipment is what I shall call 'the thought-signifying assumption'. Actually, there are two assumptions: first, that what is said (discourse) has meaning in virtue of signifying what is thought, and, secondly, that thoughts consist of ideas connected together.

One route to this assumption can begin with a remark by Plato about how thinking and discourse are related: 'Thinking and discourse are the same thing, except that what we call thinking is . . . the inward dialogue carried on by the mind with itself without spoken sound . . . whereas the stream which flows from the mind through the lips with sound is called discourse' (*Sophist* 263e). Roughly, thinking is soundless discourse, talking to oneself.

The next step is the thought that, for there to be thinking, talking to oneself is not enough. The talker-to-himself needs to understand, to know the meaning of, what he says to himself. This is his having an 'idea', which is what the words 'signify' and 'express'. As Descartes puts it:

> *Idea.* I understand this term to mean the form of any given thought, immediate perception of which makes me aware of the thought. Hence, whenever I express something in words, and understand what I am saying, this very fact makes it certain that there is within me an idea of what is signified by the words in question (Descartes, [1641] 1985, vol. II, p. 113).

It is not clear from this definition whether Descartes thought of an idea as being what is signified by a whole sentence, or of there being an idea to correspond to each word, or phrase, in the sentence. It became clearer, in the writings of Locke, that an idea was meant to be the meaning of a word or phrase, rather than of a whole sentence. Locke wrote, for example, of the idea of power. Hume followed Locke in this; he wrote of the idea of necessary connection.

(5) Hume's fifth piece of equipment is the deep metaphysical assumption to which Immanuel Kant (1724–1804) referred when he said, in the Preface to the second edition of his *Critique of Pure Reason*, 'Hitherto it has been assumed that all our knowledge must conform to objects' (Kant, [1787] 1933, B.xvi). I shall call it 'the conformity assumption'.

In the second half of the twentieth century the conformity assumption can best be explained by first distinguishing between what can be said, truly or falsely, *in* a language, and *the language* in which it is said. Consider the vocabulary of colour. Suppose that people in some alien culture (that is, where the forms of life are significantly different from ours) call two things different colours which we call the same colour. Suppose, for example, that Eskimos call fresh snow one colour, and snow that is sufficiently hard-packed to support the weight of a man without snow-shoes, a different colour, whereas we call them both the same colour, 'white'. Consider, now, the following question: Are what we call the same colour and the· Eskimos call different colours *really* the same or different? In other words, which language is right?

I can now say what it is to make the conformity assumption. Someone who makes it is someone who assumes that the question: 'Which language is right?' is meaningful, and so can have a true or false answer. Someone who makes the conformity assumption is likely to assume that his own language is right (or, in the preferred terminology, 'conforms to reality'). I call it an 'assumption', rather than a 'belief', because he may never consciously entertain the notion of language conforming, or not conforming, to reality. It is only when some part of his language strikes him as somehow unwarrantable that he says, of that part, that there is no reality to which it conforms, thereby implying that the rest of his language does conform to reality.

Kant's example of an unwarrantable part of our language is our talk of 'fortune' and 'fate'. He says that *fortune* and *fate* are 'usurpatory concepts ... which, though allowed to circulate by almost universal indulgence, are yet from time to time challenged by the question: *quid juris*' (Kant, [1787] 1933, B.117).

The significance of a concept being what Kant calls 'usurpatory' is that a sentence in which the concept is employed (such as 'He was fated to fall under a bus') is, strictly speaking, neither true nor false, but meaningless. In other words, for what is said *in* a language to be true or false, *the language* must conform to reality. And since one can be said to have knowledge only of what is true, one can have knowledge only if one's language conforms to reality. This goes some way to explaining Kant's formulation of the conformity assumption, as the assumption 'that all our knowlege must conform to objects'.

I have explained the conformity assumption as an assumption about *language* and reality. For someone who makes the thought-signifying assumption it is an assumption about *thought* and reality. And for someone who assumes that thoughts consist of ideas connected together, it is an assumption about *ideas* and reality. In the terminology favoured by Locke, ideas are either *'real'*, or *'fantastical* or *chimerical'* (Locke, [1690] 1975, II.xxx.1). They are *real* if they 'agree to the reality of things', *fantastical* or *chimerical* if they do not. Roughly, a Lockean fantastical idea corresponds to a Kantian usurpatory concept.

(6) Anyone who assumes that his ideas must be either real or fantastical cannot rest content with that assumption. He is inevitably faced with the question: how can I tell whether some idea I have is real or not? In this connection, Kant adopted the language of jurists, and talked of a 'deduction'. A 'deduction' of the concept of fate would be a proof of the 'objective reality' of fate. The trouble is that in the case of fortune and fate we cannot conceive of a suitable deduction. Kant says, about the demand for a deduction in the case of fortune and fate, the following:

> This demand for a deduction involves us in considerable perplexity, no clear legal title, sufficient to justify their employment, being obtainable either from experience or from reason (Kant, [1787] 1933, B.117).

Up until Kant brilliantly thought up what he called a 'transcendental' deduction of certain concepts, it was assumed that any deduction must be, in Kant's words, 'from experience or from reason'. Just such an assumption is Hume's fifth piece of equipment. He assumed that the proof of the reality of the idea of a necessary connection between cause and effect must be either from experience or from reason, but he rejected an alleged proof from experience and an alleged proof from reason.

The proof from experience Hume rejected is Locke's claim that we come by our idea of active power through finding 'in ourselves a *power* to begin or forbear, continue or end several actions of our minds and motions of our bodies, barely by a thought or preference of the mind ordering or, as it were commanding, the doing or not doing such or such a particular action' (Locke, [1690] 1975, II.xxi.5). Locke evidently thought that our idea of active power must be a real idea since we actually experience active power inwardly. Hume agrees that we are conscious of the motion of our body following upon the command of our will, but says that we are quite ignorant of *how* the will has the desired effect:

> The motion of our body follows upon the command of our will. Of this we are every moment conscious. But the means, by which this is effected; the energy, by which the will performs so extraordinary an operation; of this we are so far from being immediately conscious, that it must forever escape our most diligent enquiry (Hume, [1748] 1975, p. 65).

The proof from reason Hume rejected is that of Malebranche (1638–1715). Malebranche's reasoning went something like this. If some being were omnipotent then it would only have to will something to happen for it to happen. Omnipotence is such that if an omnipotent being willed something to happen it could not but happen. In other words, if 'X' is an omnipotent being, and 'Y' is the event in question, then 'X wills Y' *entails* 'Y happens'. Now, God exists, and is omnipotent, and is the only omnipotent being. So in the case of God there is a necessary connection between a cause (God, or God willing) and an effect (whatever God wills). We think of there being a necessary connection between causes and effects and in the case of God this thought applies. In fact, it applies only in the case of God. God is the only true cause. What we ordinarily think of as causes are merely the *occasions* on which God exercises his omnipotence. They are what may be called 'occasional' causes (Malebranche, [1674–5] 1980, pp. 448–50)

Subject only to the proviso that an omnipotent being

exists, Malebranche has proved that the idea of a necessary connection between cause and effect has objective reality. But his proof is such that causal necessity is analysed as a kind of logical necessity: the only causal necessity there is is the necessary connection between cause and effect that follows from the meaning of 'omnipotence'.

Hume rejected Malebranche's proof both as a proof from reason and as a proof from experience. Malebranche had not advanced it as a proof from experience, and would probably have agreed with Hume. We do not experience God exercising his omnipotent will, so if all our ideas come directly from experience, we cannot claim to have an idea of necessary connection from experience.

Hume states his reason for rejecting the proof as a proof from reason as follows:

> Though the chain of arguments which conduct to it were ever so logical, there must arise a strong suspicion, if not an absolute assurance, that it has carried us quite beyond the reach of our faculties, when it leads to conclusions so extraordinary, and so remote from common life and experience. We are got into fairy land, long ere we have reached the last steps of our theory; and *there* we have no reason to trust our common methods of argument, or to think that our usual analogies and probabilities have any authority (Hume, [1748] 1975, p. 72).

In terms of the agent causation/event causation distinction, Malebranche's position can be characterized as a total subordination of event causation to agent causation. Hume, on the other hand, is heading towards the sort of total subordination of agent causation to event causation that one finds in Skinner. The contrast is interesting in that neither of these extreme positions can accommodate ordinary human agency.

# 3 Hume's Use of his Equipment in his Reconciling Project

The use to which Hume puts his equipment is likely to be known to most readers of this volume. I can be brief.

Hume's terminology differs slightly from Locke's. Instead of asking 'Is the idea of a necessary connection between cause and effect a real idea?', he asks 'Do we really have such an idea?'. To this question his empiricist answer is: 'Yes, if there is some impression that gives rise to it'. The only impression he can find is one which he has after a frequent repetition of two objects, when one appears and 'the mind is *determined* by custom to consider its usual attendant' (Hume, [1739] 1978, p. 156). It is an impression of the mind being determined: an inward impression, not an outward one. One might reasonably expect Hume's conclusion to be that we do not have an idea of causal necessity as something in objects; we have it only as something in minds. And this, indeed, seems to be his position in the *Treatise*:

> Upon the whole, necessity is something that exists in the mind, not in objects; nor is it possible for us ever to form the most distant idea of it, considered as a quality in bodies. Either we have no idea of necessity, or necessity is nothing but that determination of the thought to pass from causes to effects and from effects to causes, according to their experienced union (Hume, [1739] 1978, pp. 165–6).

In the first *Enquiry*, however, Hume formulates his conclusion differently: the necessity we ascribe to matter (or 'conceive in matter') is wholly comprised by the constant conjunction of two objects, and the consequent inference of the mind from one to the other (Hume, [1748] 1975, pp. 82, 92–3, 96, 96n.). This is a bit like saying that there *is* necessity in matter, but that it is *nothing but* a constant conjunction of objects and consequent inference of the mind. Why should Hume want to say that there is necessity in matter? Possibly because he likes to be able to agree with what he thinks is 'universally allowed', and he thinks 'it is universally allowed that matter, in all its operations, is actuated by a necessary force, and that every natural effect is so precisely determined by the energy of its cause that no other effect, in such particular circumstances, could possibly have resulted from it' (ibid., p. 82). Since he wants to agree with this, he transforms the original question 'Do we have an idea of a necessary connection in matter?' If he had stuck with the original question, and given the answer 'No' he could hardly have agreed with what he says is universally allowed. With the transformed question, and the answer 'Constant conjunction and consequent inference', he can just about get away with agreeing with it. It is a bit like being asked whether one agrees with what is universally allowed, that physical objects have an objective (mind-independent) existence; one can just about get away with the answer 'Yes, though their objective existence consists in the fact that anyone in the right place will have sensations of them'.

Hume, intent upon reconciling liberty and necessity, next brings his 'constant conjunction and consequent inference' analysis of causal necessity to bear on his notion that there is a constant conjunction of motives and actions (his second piece of equipment). The bearing of it is obvious: in the only allowable sense of 'necessitate', motives necessitate actions. This, then, is the necessity that has to be shown to be compatible with liberty. But liberty simply is an agent's having 'a power of acting, or not acting, according to the determinations of the will' (his third piece of equipment). If the second part of this means 'according to how the will is determined', and it is granted that the will is determined by motives, then Hume is home and dry. Indeed, liberty and necessity are not merely compatible, they are *the same thing*: the determination of the will by motives.

# 4 The Essence of Necessity

Let me briefly recapitulate. Hume made the conformity assumption. In Kantian terminology, he 'assumed that all our knowledge must conform to objects'. He applied the assumption to our idea of causal necessity. Do we know, either from reason or from experience, that our idea of causal necessity has an objective counterpart? He rejected Malebranche's theory that we know from reason (that is, from analysing the notion of omnipotence) that there is objective causal necessity at least (and at most) in the case of *God willing* things, on the ground that 'we are got into fairy land, long ere we have reached the last steps of our theory', and on the ground that we do not experience God willing. He rejected Locke's theory that we know from experience (that is, from the experience of *our willing* having effect), on the ground that we do not know the means by which our willing has its effect. He propounded an empiricist theory of his own, one which led him to conclude that 'beyond the constant *conjunction* of similar objects, and the consequent *inference* from one to the other, we have no notion of any necessity or connexion' (Hume, [1748] 1975, p. 82). In brief, 'this constancy forms the very essence of necessity' (ibid., p. 96n.).

The next question is: how does Hume's statement of the essence of causal necessity measure up to our actual practice with the word 'cause'? There are numerous cases in which one object is constantly followed by another, so that on perceiving one we can confidently expect the other. According to Hume, we should call the first the cause of the second. Do we?

In a wide sense of 'object', day is an object that is constantly followed by night. And nobody doubts that if it is daytime, night is coming. There is 'constant conjunction and consequent inference'. But do we say that day is the cause of night? No.

I have chosen this example, rather than that of the two ideal clocks (Flew, 1982, p. 490), because of the significance of what we *do* say. Day is not the cause of night, but day and night are causally connected. Night follows day because (causal 'because') the earth revolves on its axis. In other words, *if* the earth were to stop revolving on its axis the succession of day and night would stop.

It is the 'if' that is significant. As John Stuart Mill put it, in a masterly understatement, 'if a person eats of a particular dish, and dies in consequence, that is, would not have died if he had not eaten of it, people would be apt to say that eating of that dish was the cause of his death' (Mill, [1843] 1974, III.v.3). It is part of what we mean when we say that X causes Y that *if* X were to happen Y would happen, this being something we can say even if X does not happen. Even if the earth does not stop revolving on its axis we can say that *if* it were to stop so would the succession of day and night. To adapt to my own purposes an expression used by the Oxford philosopher J. L. Austin (1911–60), causation is constitutionally *iffy*.

Now, Hume's remark that 'constancy forms the very essence of necessity' ignores this. It suggests that we find out what causes what by passively registering sequences of events and allowing them to form habits of expectation in our minds. But we cannot find out that *if* the earth were to stop revolving on its axis the succession of night and day would stop by passively registering sequences of events (unless, of course, the earth *were* to stop revolving on its axis – though, if it were, we would probably not be in a position to register anything). In short, to find out what causes what it is not enough passively to register sequences of events; one needs to be active, to think up possible causal explanations, devise experiments to test them, conduct the experiments and draw conclusions from the results. This, and not the passive registration of sequences of events, is the actual causal practice in which we engage. And it is a practice that is not suggested by Hume's definition of 'cause' in so far as the definition expresses his empiricist answer to the question 'What precisely is our idea of a necessary connection in matter?'

It needs to be added that Hume is not above misrepresenting his answer to this question, so as to accommodate the *iffy* nature of causation. Thus he writes:

> . . . we may define a cause to be *an object, followed by another, and when all the objects similar to the first are followed by objects similar to the second. Or in other* words, *where, if the first object had not been, the second never had existed* (Hume, [1748] 1975, p. 76).

The first part of this definition (the part before 'in other words') expresses his empiricist theory of causation. The second part does not. The first part suggests we would call day the cause of night, because days always are followed by nights. The second part suggests that we would call the revolution of the earth on its axis the cause of the succession of day and night, because if the earth had not revolved on its axis the succession would not have existed. Hume's empiricist answer to the question 'What precisely is our idea of a necessary connection in matter?' does not entitle him to the second part. He has helped himself to it, in order to make it appear that, once again, he is saying what would be universally acknowledged. But the empiricist part is very far from being generally acceptable. As Flew put it: '. . . we cannot protest either too soon or too often that what Hume is offering is in truth not so much a fresh account of the meaning of the word "necessity", as, rather, a denial that there is any such thing as that to which that word, as previously understood, pretended to refer' (p. 73).

## 5  Back to Antony Flew

At the beginning of his first contribution Flew said he would have to reserve his remarks about physical determination until after I had declared my own intentions. I have not yet done so. But I have prepared the ground for doing so – in particular, by drawing attention to the role, in philosophizing about causal necessity, of the conformity assumption. An understanding of the conformity assumption is, in my view, the key to understanding the peculiar metaphysical status of physical determinism. And such an understanding is, I believe, the route to an alternative, and more acceptable, compatibilism.

The questions now before my mind are the following. Does Flew, like Hume, make the conformity assumption? Does he, making it, agree with Hume that we get the idea of necessity from experience? Does he disagree with Hume only about what the relevant experience is? Hume thought it is the experience of the mind being determined by custom to consider one object upon the perception of another with which it has been constantly conjoined. Does Flew think that it is, instead, the experience of finding, as Edwards puts it, in early childhood, that there are 'innumerable things that can't be done', and innumerable things that 'will be whether they choose them or no' (p. 68)?

If Flew has, like Hume, made the conformity assumption, and has, like Hume, opted for the 'from experience' answer to the question 'How can I tell whether some idea I have is real or not?', what impact, if any, has my bringing the conformity assumption out into the open had on him? Have I succeeded, or failed, in making clear what the assumption is? It would not be surprising if I have failed, for it is a singularly deep metaphysical assumption. In short, I think we may be on the brink of a 'really substantial disagreement', or, if not a disagreement exactly, at least a lack of mutual understanding.

# In the Second Round

ANTONY FLEW

# 1  A Short, Sharp First Reply

I shall begin by giving curt and dogmatic answers to the questions which Godfrey Vesey has just posed at the end of his second contribution; move next to what he said at the beginning of that contribution; and only after that proceed to a more thorough, argued response to those questions. This will take the discussion up again at precisely the point of strategic promise where Vesey left off. For I believe it to be no accident that it was as a result of years of critical study of Hume that I myself reached my present conclusions about these matters; while these conclusions themselves are, surely, also best expounded by reference to the insights and errors of 'le bon David'.

(1) Question one: 'Does Flew, like Hume, make the conformity assumption?' Yes, he most certainly does. For how could anyone who is serious and sincere in the pursuit of knowledge fail to insist that not just 'all our knowledge', but absolutely and without qualification *all* knowledge of *objects* 'must conform to objects'? To know something about some objects simply is to know that that something is true of those objects; while thus 'to be true of', is, presumably, what is meant here by 'conforming to'. (The reason for limiting the claim to knowledge of *objects* is to bypass disputes about whether the logically necessary truths of pure mathematics are, as Plato at one stage seems to have thought, truths about a special sort of out-of-this-worldly mathematical objects.)

(2) Question two: Does Flew, making this modest though altogether fundamental conformity assumption, 'agree with Hume that we get the idea of necessity from experience? Does he disagree with Hume only about what the experience is?' Again the answer is a most emphatic 'Yes!'.

Here it is important to distinguish two crucially different

senses of the key term 'experience'. In the ordinary, everyday sense a claim to have had experience of something is a claim to have been in direct contact with mind-independent realities; whereas Hume is officially committed to the contentions that he, and we, are never so privileged as to be granted any such close and cognitive contacts with an or the External World. He, therefore, is entitled to employ the word 'experience', and all other terms with similar meanings, with reference only to ongoings in his own mind – to his own Internal World, so to speak.

To bring out the enormous and vital difference between these two senses, consider the sad case of the philosophically scrupulous applicant who responds to the advertisement of a farmer seeking to hire hands 'with experience of cows'. In interview he, or she, has to admit that – despite having had both many dreams of cows and abundant cowish sense-data – he, or she, neither is nor ever will be in a position to know that there even are such things as cows. Such an applicant would be lucky simply to be dismissed from interview, without suffering any penalty for impertinence.

Given this important distinction between the factitious, philosophical, logically private understanding of the word 'experience' and its ordinary, everyday, essentially cognitive meaning, we have to distinguish two corresponding senses of 'empiricism'. Taking 'based upon or derived from' to be the core idea, the thesis of logical empiricism becomes the claim that all knowledge – or, rather, all knowledge of contingent facts – must be somehow referred to experience. If 'experience' is then construed in the ordinary sense, logical empiricism becomes, surely, a truism; albeit a truism of the last importance? But if the same word is construed in the mind-dependent, private sense, then verbally the same doctrine becomes, though perennially fascinating, ultimately – or perhaps not so ultimately – preposterous. Hume's philosophical empiricism is, of course, of this second sort, since his 'ideas and impressions' – the two kinds of 'perceptions of the mind' – are two kinds of experience (philosophical). So when 'I agree with Hume that we get the idea of necessity from experience', he and I are not interpreting the key term in the same way. He sought a (private) impression from which the idea of necessity might be derived. What I believe I have found is experience of practical necessity and practical impossibility as altogether familiar, mind-independent realities.

(3) Vesey's third question concerns the nature of the experience which I believe I have found: 'Does Flew think that it is, instead, the experience of finding, in early childhood, that there are 'innumerable things that can't be done', and innumerable things that 'will be whether they choose them or no'? Yes, indeed, I do believe that it is this experience, which is of a kind familiar to us all from our earliest days.

(4) Vesey's final question refers to the conformity assumption: 'Have I succeeded, or failed, in making clear what the assumption is?' It is, I think, for him to tell me, in the light of my response to his first question. I hesitate. My first inclination was to return another categorical 'Yes!'. But then it occurred to me that if my understanding were correct then this becomes an assumption that cannot sensibly be challenged. Nor is it one which anyone could deserve much credit either for noticing or for spelling out. Yet Vesey seems to think, on the contrary: first, that what he has in mind in speaking of the conformity assumption might be challenged, reasonably if not perhaps in the end rightly; and, second, that an explanation of its mysteries is 'the route to an alternative, and more acceptable, compatibilism' (p. 114). Since I shall soon be putting my incompatibilist cards on the table, this 'conformity assumption' is clearly something about which Vesey must tell us more.

## 2  A Miscellany of Points

About Skinner's project for an unanthropomorphic science of man, and about the importance of the issues in dispute between ourselves and Skinner, Vesey and I are completely agreed. But I will add two things before moving on, and perhaps apart. First, Skinner has his own perverse and peculiar 'conformity assumption'. It is: not that every science must conform to whatever are the facts in its particular field; but that the nature of man must be such as to make possible the fulfilment of his own perversely chosen, blinkered programme. 'I deny that freedom exists at all. I must deny it – or my programme would be absurd.' Could this quotation from *Walden Two* (Skinner, 1948) be better capped than with the words of Groucho Marx: 'It looks absurd. But don't be misled. It is absurd'?

The second addendum comes from Leszek Kolakowski, who has as good a reason as any to know how formidable are the threats to political freedoms coming from followers of another, much less entertaining Marx:

> Our hope that freedom is not going to be ultimately destroyed by the joint pressure of totalitarianism and the general bureaucratization of the world, and indeed our very readiness to defend it, depends crucially on our belief that the desire for freedom . . . is not an accidental fancy of history, not a result of peculiar social conditions or a temporary by-product of specific economic life forms . . . but that it is rooted in the very quality of being human.

In my first contribution I claimed: 'It is for many purposes fruitful to see Plato and Aristotle as the Founding Fathers of two rival traditions about the nature of man . . . ' (p. 49). Vesey enters reservations on two counts, and on both counts he is quite right. I must, therefore, explain myself more fully. First, Vesey suggests that it may be misleading to attach the label 'Platonic–Cartesian' to one of these two traditions. But his reason for objecting is at the same time my reason for saying 'Platonic–Cartesian' rather than, simply, 'Platonic'. By making consciousness the essential, defining characteristic of his incorporeal soul, Descartes gave a sharp new turn to the dualist tradition, which originally stemmed from Plato.

Second, whereas Plato is almost always a thoroughgoing Platonist, Aristotle is scarcely ever, unreservedly Aristotelian! So wherever it is – as it so often is – pedagogically profitable to make a Platonic/Aristotelian contrast, we usually find something in Aristotle which for that purpose has to be in some way discounted. In the present case that something is, as Vesey indicates, Aristotle's incongruous and doubtfully intelligible doctrine of the immortality of the non-personal and non-individual intellect.

In section 2 of his first contribution Vesey expounded a crucial and fundamental distinction made first and very well by Plato (see pp. 7–12). In my response (pp. 55–6) I faulted Vesey for adopting for the two terms of this distinction the labels 'agent causation and event causation', though I allowed that these expressions were at least preferable to the '*immanent* causation' and '*transeunt* causation' preferred by Chisholm. My objection was – and is – that this 'is bound to suggest that the distinction is between different sorts of causing rather than different senses of (the word) "cause" ' (p. 55). That this is what it is indeed bound to suggest is – I still believe – made very clear by my subsequent quotation from Chisholm: 'I shall say that when one event . . . causes some other event . . . then we have an instance of *transeunt* causation. And I shall say that when an *agent*, as distinguished from an event, causes an event . . . , then we have an instance of *immanent* causation' (p. 55).

From this I proceeded to insist that when two possible causes, one a human action and the other a natural occurrence, bring about the same effect, they both make it happen, both physically necessitate its occurrence. they are, therefore, both causes of the same sort and causes in the same sense. What puzzled Vesey is that I then went on to say: 'The enormously important difference, and hence the right distinction, lies between: on the one hand, the sense in which an agent is said *to be caused* to act; and, on the other hand, the sense in which anything else is said *to be caused* to occur' (p. 56). The wrong distinction is that between *causing by* an agent and *causing by* an event; and it is wrong because there is in truth no difference to be distinguished between these supposed two sorts of causing, supposed two senses of 'cause'. The right distinction is the right distinction because it distinguishes the enormous and crucial difference obtaining between two actual sorts of cause, two actual senses of 'cause': the one necessarily involves physical necessitation; the other, with an equal necessity, must incline but cannot similarly necessitate.

I do not, however, regret that Vesey was for a time perplexed by what I wrote. For it was worth making two points which otherwise he might not have made. One was that 'people do often act without any thought of ends to be achieved' (p. 98); ends other, that is, than the ends of satisfying desires so to act – an operation sometimes confused with the pursuit of pleasure. The other was that talk of motives sometimes falsely suggests external forces irresistibly impelling agents to act (p. 98).

Attempting to explain what he means by 'the conformity assumption', Vesey asks us to consider:

> the vocabulary of colour. Suppose that people in some alien culture (that is, where the forms of life are significantly different from ours) call two things different colours which we call the same colour. Suppose, for example, that Eskimos call fresh snow one colour, and snow that is sufficiently hard-packed to support the weight of a man without snow-shoes, a different colour, whereas we call them both the same colour, 'white' (pp. 104–5).

The questions which Vesey wants us to answer – after due consideration – are: 'Are what we call the same colour and the Eskimos call different colours *really* the same or different? In other words, which language is right?' But here the briefest of considerings leads me to the perhaps too hasty conclusion that this case constitutes no reason whatsoever for believing that either English or Inuit is either right or wrong. What the case as described surely shows, quite decisively, is: that the words which the Inuit use to mark a visually perceived difference between fresh-fallen and hard-packed snow are not words for colours; and that the presumption to beat is that they are words for precisely that visually perceivable difference which we too are able to discern but which – for obvious reasons – English is not so well equipped to mark?

Perhaps I have totally failed to grasp what Vesey is driving at when he writes about 'the conformity assumption'. But what is certain is that the present example provides no illumination. For it embodies, and is vitiated by, its own fatal, false assumption. This is that we can have to the meanings of words in some strange language an access wholly independent of any study of the occasions upon which native speakers employ or refuse to employ those words. It is as if it was believed that the standard English–Inuit/Inuit–English dictionary – if such there be – had come down from the heavens, endowed with inexpugnable authority. Many, indeed, of the participants in recent debates about rationality or irrationality among primitive peoples appear to have been clients to similarly superstitious assumptions (Flew, 1976, ch. 3).

Vesey refers to section 41 of *The Principles of Philosophy*, in which Descartes attempts to show 'How to reconcile the freedom of our will with divine preordination'. Very correctly Vesey comments: 'I do not think that the content of the section lives up to the title, and I cannot think of anything that would do so' (p. 100). On this Vesey and I are, of course, in complete agreement. But it is, for two reasons, worth adding something about Hume's treatment of the same question: first, because until very recently everyone – starting with Hume himself – seems to have missed its true implications; and, second, because sorting this out is a good way of underlining some fundamental truths about the relations, and lack of relations, between agency and necessity.

Hume deals with this question in Part II of the section 'Of Liberty and Necessity' in the first *Enquiry*. It is a discussion which has no substantial predecessor in the *Treatise* as published. In this Part II Hume pretends to be dealing, as best he can, with supposedly formidable difficulties for the compatibilist 'reconciling project' of Part I. The reality is that his dealings are all an exercise in intellectual judo, in which Hume skilfully turns the impetus of a hostile charge into a means for enforcing the chief desired conclusion of the entire *Enquiry concerning Human Understanding*:

> To reconcile the indifference and contingency of human actions with prescience; or to defend absolute decrees, and yet free the Deity from being the author of sin, has been found hitherto to exceed all the power of philosophy. Happy, if she be thence sensible of her temerity, . . . and . . . return with suitable modesty, to her true and proper province, the examination of common life (Hume, [1748] 1975, VIII.ii, p. 103).

This characteristically swinging and mischievous enterprise is, however, fundamentally flawed. Very reasonably, Hume insists that all reward and punishment must presuppose that the persons to be so treated are the causes of whatever it is for which they are to be rewarded or punished. (Not so reasonably, and entirely by the way, he appears further to require that their actions be in character, (ibid., p. 98). He then entertains what ironically he presents as an objection 'to this theory with regard to necessity and liberty':

> It may be said, for instance, that if voluntary actions be subjected to the same laws of necessity with the operations of matter, there is a continued chain of necessary causes, pre-ordained and pre-determined, reaching from the original cause of all to every single volition of every human creature (ibid., p. 99).

Thus, Hume continues, speaking of God, 'He foresaw, he ordained, he intended all those actions of men which we so rashly pronounce criminal. And we must, therefore, conclude either that they are not criminal or that the Deity, not man, is accountable for them' (ibid., p. 100).

Of these two options Hume rules out the first on what is for him the congenial, radically secular and humanist ground that 'these distinctions are founded in the natural sentiments of the human mind . . . not to be controlled or altered by any philosophical theory or speculation whatsoever' (ibid., p. 103). The second is, therefore chosen. But it is construed as justifying the equally congenial, equally secular moral that philosophy should confine herself to the proper province of the human understanding, the study of human nature and human affairs, 'without launching into so boundless an ocean of doubt, uncertainty and contradiction' (ibid., p. 103).

What even those interpreters who appreciate Hume's irony have failed to recognize is that this pretended objection both in fact and necessarily construes causation in a sense much stronger than any for which Hume can make provision. Thus the penultimate passage quoted in the last paragraph but one has to continue, immediately:

> No contingency anywhere in the universe, no indifference, no liberty. While we act, we are at the same time acted upon. The ultimate Author of all our volitions is the Creator of the world, who first bestowed motion on this immense machine and placed all beings in that particular position whence every subsequent event, by an inevitable necessity, must result (ibid., p. 99–100).

We categorically cannot read this talk of 'an inevitable necessity' in Hume's official, denatured sense. For liberty, as he has himself been arguing in Part I, is completely compatible with necessity, in 'a new sense of necessity'. But in the present passage divine causality specifically leaves no room whatsoever for alternatives, 'no liberty'. So what in Part II is supposed to be the particular application of the reconciling ideas of Part I is in fact inconsistent with them. The objection with which Hume, as an aggressive agnostic, hopes to devastate theism must itself collapse if Hume's account of causation is correct. Yet, if that account is to be accepted in its entirety, then atheists too must be involved in a common ruin.

The crux is that the notion of agency, whether human or divine, itself contains and implies much more than that brute fact constant and merely successive conjunction, which is all that Hume can admit into causation as a philosophical relation. In the *Abstract* he concludes, in a picturesque trope, that the principles of the association of ideas 'are really *to us* the cement of the universe' (Hume, [1740] 1978, p. 662). But for him the corollary is and must be that the universe *in itself*, outwith the human mind, has no cement at all; everything is 'entirely loose and separate'.

Doing, however, is a kind of causing, of making something happen. Such a Humian universe will, therefore, be one in which nothing at all is ever actually done. There are, that is to say, no basic actions such that something else would not have happened if they had not. Nothing is ever made either practically impossible or practically inevitable, whether by human agency or by God. All there are, are universal regularities in the occurrence of successive events which are in themselves entirely loose, separate and unconnected.

So Hume is not entitled to help himself to that comfortable teaching against 'launching into so boundless an ocean of doubt, uncertainty, and contradiction'. If the theologians were to accept Hume's reductive reinterpretation of the necessity of causes, then they could spare their God the charge of being the ultimate author of sin. But then they, like the rest of us, would benefit from that reductive reinterpretation only at the altogether unacceptable price of maintaining that no one, whether God or man, actually brings about anything at all. For in a strictly Humian universe there is no room for either necessity or agency, whether human or divine.

# 3 Agency and Necessity as Experienced Realities

The second two sections of Vesey's second contribution deal with 'Hume's equipment', and with the use of 'this equipment in his reconciling project'. It is curious that Vesey's inventory does not list the three Cartesian presuppositions which – as I have argued at length elsewhere (Flew, 1986) – condition most of Hume's distinctive insights and errors. His three presuppositions all combine to prevent Hume from recognizing that, and how, we can and cannot but acquire these crucial, complementary concepts from our own immediate and ever-renewed experience of the realities to which they refer; or which are, if you prefer, their objects.

At the beginning of Part IV of his *Discourse on the Method*, after a smoothly discursive build-up in the suave and apparently innocuous Parts I–III, Descartes suddenly releases a shattering salvo of almost all-destroying doubt. Just as Goethe, who was present, said that the cannonade of Valmy opened a new era in human history, so, with equal truth, it can be asserted that the modern period in philosophy starts with this single devastating sentence:

> Thus, because our senses sometimes deceive us, I wished to suppose that nothing is just as they cause us to imagine it to be, and because there are men who deceive themselves in their reasoning, and fall into paralogisms . . . judging that I was as subject to error as any other, I rejected as false all the reasons formerly accepted by me as demonstrations.

So, because (? we know that) we are sometimes mistaken in our judgements about the furniture of the universe around us, and conceivably always might be, perhaps we never really know anything about what is the case there; and, because (? we know that) we have sometimes been mistaken about the validity of inferences, and conceivably always might be, perhaps we can never truly identify any argument as valid or any demonstration as genuine.

Next Descartes proceeds to pick out what alone seems to remain of rock-solid certainty: 'But immediately afterwards I noticed that whilst I thus wished to think all things false, it was absolutely essential that the "I" who thought this should be somewhat . . . '. Hence 'this truth, "*I think therefore I am*" ' became 'so certain and so assured that all the most extravagant suppositions brought forward by the sceptics were incapable of shaking it . . . '.

It is important to recognize that for Descartes the word 'thought' has, officially, a much wider than usual signification. It covers, not only the activity in which Rodin's *Le Penseur* is engaged, but also the enjoying or not enjoying of any and every form of consciousness – including the suffering of pains which may make ratiocination impossible. This comes out most clearly in his definitions of 'thought' and 'idea' in a passage from which Vesey found reason to quote in both his contributions (pp. 16–17, 104). These Cartesian thoughts are the ideas of Locke's 'new way of ideas', and hence the ideas of Berkeley too. They are Hume's 'perceptions of the mind', by him subdivided into 'ideas and impressions'. And subsequently they have become the peculiarly private experiences of later philosophers.

Having discovered that 'this truth, "*I think therefore I am*" ' was 'so certain and so assured that all the most extravagant suppositions brought forward by the sceptics were incapable of shaking it', the next step was that of 'examining attentively that which I was'. This examination led Descartes to conclude:

> that I was a substance the whole essence or nature of which is to think, that for its existence there is no need of any place, nor does it depend on any material thing; so that this 'me', that is to say, the soul by which I am what I am, is entirely distinct from body . . .; and even if body were not, the soul would not cease to be what it is.

We are now in a position to distinguish three main elements in this so seductively presented Cartesian vision. All three are assumptions that Hume took to be 'the obvious dictates of reason', which 'no man, who reflects, ever doubted'; although it was to only one of them – the second – that he directed these explicit words (Hume, [1748] 1975, XII.i, p. 152). First comes the assumption that all arguments must be either deductive or defective, since the only sufficient reasons for believing any proposition are (other) propositions which entail it. Second is the notion that we are (all of us) forever imprisoned behind Veils of Appearance, since it is supposed that we can never be immediately aware of any mind-independent realities. Third, and finally, it is argued or assumed that we essentially are either incorporeal subjects of or even nothing else but collections of (only) the limited and ingrown sort of experiences allowed for under the second of these three principles.

In my first contribution I quoted a curt, crushing, single-sentence paragraph from the *Treatise*: 'The distinction, which we often make betwixt *power* and the *exercise* of it, is . . . without foundation' (p. 76). Perhaps it is less than instantly obvious what this most categorical assertion is supposed to be denying. Some slight light is to be found in the rather unexpected context of a discussion 'Of property and riches'. In that essay Hume maintains:

> . . . Since therefore we ascribe a power of performing an action to every one, who has no very powerful motive to forbear it, and refuse it to such as have; it may justly be concluded, that *power* has always a reference to its *exercise*, either actual or probable, and that we consider a person as endow'd with any ability, when we find from past experience, that 'tis probable, or at least possible that he may exert it (Hume, [1741–77] 1985, p. 313).

What we need here is another very important and fundamental distinction; a distinction between, if you like, a physical and a moral or personal power. Physical powers are possessed by or attributed to inanimate objects; and powers of this kind are indeed definable, as Hume urges, in terms of the actual or possible behaviour of those objects to which they are attributed. This is the sense in which one speaks of the brake horsepower of a car, or of the explosive power of what at one time was rather prissily known as 'a nuclear device'. The second sense, the sense in which Hume in the *Treatise* wanted to deny that there is any such thing, is that of a personal power. It is in this understanding that it might be somewhat unfashionably said that J. V. Stalin possessed the power of life or death – or much worse – over every single subject of what we should nowadays be reproached for describing as 'the evil empire'. Failure to make and maintain this distinction was responsible for much of the confusion in, and between, and arising from, the *First Essay* and the *Second Essay* of Malthus (Flew, 1984, ch. 4); and compare Flew, 1978, ch. 2).

To possess such a personal power is to be able, at will, either to have or to do whatever it is the power to acquire or to achieve. Whatever people possessing such a personal power choose to do, it has to be true too that, in some strong sense, they could have done otherwise. In order to achieve a better understanding, both of what that sense is and of why Hume denied that it could have any application, we need to make another, more constructive review of the great chapter 'Of Power' in Locke's *Essay*. Certainly Hume makes it very clear that it is primarily this document which he is criticizing in both his treatments 'Of the Idea of necessary Connexion'.

It is unfortunate that in these critiques Hume does not let Locke speak for himself. Speaking for him, Hume proposes: 'It may be said that we are every moment conscious of internal power; while we feel, that by simple command of our will, we can move the organs of our body, or direct the faculties of our mind. . . . This influence of the will we know by consciousness' (Hume, [1748] 1975, VII.ii, p. 64). As Vesey says, Descartes had played into Hume's hands 'by inventing acts of will' (p. 102; and compare p. 16 and section 3 of Vesey's first contribution).

The nub of Hume's objection is put in a single sentence: 'This influence we may observe, is a fact, which like all other natural events, can be known only by experience, and can never be foreseen from any apparent energy or power in the cause, which connects it with the effect, and renders the one an infallible consequence of the other' (pp. 64–5).

To understand both the objection itself, and why the answer provided is believed to be decisive, we have to recognize that both challenge and response take our three Cartesian presuppositions for granted. This recognition is handicapped by the inclusion of a scandalously inconsistent, grossly unsceptical reference to knowledge in the definition of 'will' in the *Treatise*: 'I desire it may be observ'd, that by the *will*, I mean nothing but the *internal impression we feel and are conscious of, when we knowingly give rise to any new motion of our body, or new perception of our mind*' (Hume, [1739] 1978, II.iii.1, p. 399).

Hume underlines his intention to refer to a putative impression – a kind of Cartesian 'thought', such as might possibly be had by an incorporeal subject of consciousness – by adding at once: 'This impression ... [Surprise, surprise!] ... 'tis impossible to define, and needless to describe any farther'. Remembering both the first of Hume's three Cartesian principles and what Vesey has written about the Cartesian invention of 'acts of will', it becomes obvious that Hume cannot allow the occurrence of such 'thoughts' to constitute sufficient grounds for claims to know the consequences thereof.

Suppose now that we look for ourselves at how Locke tried to explain the notion of power. Certainly he too was handicapped by the same Cartesian presuppositions. But if we are not, then we can find Locke's contribution most helpfully suggestive. At first his words are very like those which Hume puts into his mouth:

This at least I think evident. That we find in our selves a *Power* to begin or forbear, continue or end several actions of our minds, and motions of our Bodies, barely by a thought or preference of the mind ordering, or as it were commanding the doing or not doing such or such a particular action. This *power* is that which we call the *Will* ([1690] 1975, II.xxi. 5, p. 236).

Soon, however, it is a different and better story; marred only by the fact that Locke sees himself as spelling out what is meant by 'a free agent' rather than, more simply and more fundamentally, by 'an agent' or – and, surely, tautologically? – 'a choosing agent'. (The three Latin words refer to St Vitus's dance.) Locke is now contrasting cases in which power is lacking:

We have instances enough, and often more than enough in our own Bodies. A Man's Heart beats, and the Blood circulates, which 'tis not in his Power . . . to stop; and therefore in respect of these Motions, where rest depends not on his choice . . . he is not a *free Agent*. Convulsive Motions agitate his Legs, so that though he wills it never so much, he cannot . . . stop their Motion (as in that odd Disease called *chorea Sancti Viti*,) but he is perpetually dancing. He is . . . under as much Necessity of moving, as a Stone that falls, or a Tennis-ball struck with a Racket. On the other side, a Palsie or the Stocks hinder his Legs . . . (ibid., II.xxi. 7 and 11, pp. 237, 239).

I propose to maintain that Locke in this seminal passage at least suggested, even if it would perhaps be too generous to allow that he showed, that and how it is possible to provide ostensive definitions, not only of '(personal) power' but of all the other key terms and expressions also – terms and expressions such as '(choosing) agent', '(practical) necessity', or 'can (in a strong sense) do other than they do do'. It seems too that no one could ever be in a position consistently to assert, much less to know: either that there is no such thing as (unnecessitated) choice; or that there is no such thing as (practical) necessity. For it appears that choice and necessity are two opposites, of such a kind that each can be explained only by pointing to actual specimens both of its own and of the other sort. Thus anyone able to understand either of these two notions must have been acquainted with some specimens of both the two sorts of realities to which they respectively refer.

The previous paragraph contains two contentions about the particular collection of key concepts with which we are concerned, a stronger and a weaker. The weaker thesis is that all the members of this collection, a membership linked by various entailments and incompatibilities, can be ostensively defined by reference to universally familiar sorts of experience. The stronger is that these concepts could not be explained to or acquired by creatures that never enjoyed or suffered these sorts of experience. (The word 'experience' is, of course, here employed always and only in the everyday, exoteric rather than the purely philosophical, esoteric sense.)

In the nature of the case arguments for my stronger thesis are bound to be negative, citing the failure of well-girded attempts to do what that thesis maintains cannot be done. Nor is there any doubt but that the most impressive of such failures, because beyond question the most well-girded, was that of Hume. Refusing to appeal to experience of the External World, he could find in his Internal World no objects for the concepts of agent power, of practical necessity or of practical impossibility. So if anyone chooses to deny this my stronger thesis, it is up to them to falsify it by themselves developing alternative ways of explaining and legitimatizing these notions. Like the man from Missouri, I have to be shown!

To bring out how the argument for the weaker thesis must go, we have to insist on starting not with Lockean ideas or Humian 'perceptions of the mind', but with bodily movements. Let those that can be either initiated or quashed at will be labelled 'movings', and those that cannot, 'motions'. (These verbal recommendations have the merit of going with rather than against the grain of common usage.) Certainly it is obvious that there are plenty of marginal cases. Nevertheless, so long as there are, as there are, plenty – indeed far, far more – which fall unequivocally upon one side or the other, we must resolutely and stubbornly refuse to be prevented from insisting on a humanly vital distinction by any such diversionary appeals to the existence of marginal cases.

Now suppose that, for the moment, and for the sake of simplicity, we both ignore purely mental actions – such as summoning up a mental image – and refuse to make any distinction between those cases in which an agent chooses to move and those in which the choice is *not* to move. Then it becomes easy to recognize that the notions of action, of choice and (in the strong sense) of being able to do otherwise can be, and surely must be, explained by reference to what, given the previous simplifying assumptions, all actions must involve; namely, movings as distinct from motions. Vesey, in his second contribution, argued against Skinner that: 'Without the agent . . . *doing something* (in the sense of "doing something" in which a reflex response, such as salivation, is *not* doing something) there would be no behaviour to be "reinforced" by "conditioning" ' (p. 95). Doing something in my terminology involves movings, whereas reflex responses are merely motions. What makes Skinner's programme not so much unscientific as anti-scientific is that it commits him to denying the reality of agency; something altogether familiar, and at the same time fundamentally different from what is so misleadingly called 'reflex action'.

Again, given an awareness of this difference between movings and motions, it also becomes easy to appreciate – and this time with no call for any simplifying assumptions – that all of us as agents are forever engaged in confronting ourselves with both practical necessities and their complementary practical impossibilities. We do this every time we make something happen, and thereby make it impossible for it not to happen.

In that same second contribution Vesey refers to Austin's claim that ' "cans" are constitutionally "iffy" ' (p. 112). Vesey goes on to quote a now notorious passage in the first *Enquiry* (p. 113). Certainly, from a premise stating only that – as a matter of brute fact – all 'thisses' have been, are and will be followed by 'thats', we cannot validly deduce any subjunctive, counterfactual conditional such as: 'If on such and such an occasion there had been a this, which there was not, then it would have been followed by a that'. Equally certainly it is a defining characteristic of nomological propositions – a class which embraces statements both of laws of nature and of physical causes – that these propositions do carry counterfactual conditional entailments. To come down from abstract air to concrete earth, if I say that the cause of the trouble was no petrol in the tank then my statement implies that, all other things being equal, had the tank been full the machine would have started.

Now the reason why such inferences can validly be drawn from nomologicals is precisely and only that nomological propositions assert practical necessities and practical impossibilities. We know that, if the nomological is true, then if there were to have been a this it would have been followed by a that, precisely and only because the nomological itself asserts the *impossibility* of a this not being followed by a that. The very idea of counterfactual conditionality is thus by a logical necessary connection linked with those of practical necessity and practical impossibility. It is, surely, obvious that and why this is an idea which is easy for us to grasp? We are, after all, agents familiar as such with the ever-present possibility and power of doing other than we do do. Suppose we were instead creatures who were not agents possessed of personal powers and who were, therefore, never confronted with actual alternative possibilities? How could we then become seized of the concept of counterfactual conditionality; or, indeed, of any other concept whatsoever? (Does not the possibility of any correct verbal usage itself presuppose the possibility of the incorrect?)

Suppose, as I am maintaining, all these closely connected, crucial concepts are, and can only be, acquired from our familiar experience of their various objects. Then how come that Hume – the ungullible Hume, as Gilbert Ryle so loved to describe him – failed to discover these legitimating sources? In the search for some Humian impression from which 'the idea of necessary connexion' might be derived, Hume's overriding concern is to defend the insight that, 'If we reason *a priori*, anything may appear able to produce anything' (Hume, [1748] 1975, XII.iii, p. 164). So he never clearly recognizes the possibilities of a second sense of 'necessity'; of a second sort of necessity. In the second place, Hume's whole investigation is conducted within the framework provided by those three Cartesian presuppositions. So, trying to act as if he were an incorporeal subject of purely private experience, he searches for the impression from which a not specifically practical idea of necessary connection might have been derived. Then, by appealing to the first of his three Cartesian principles, all the few candidates presenting themselves for examination are promptly disqualified. For it must remain always conceivable that the having of any particular candidate impression will in fact be followed by some occurrence other than whatever its actual practical consequence is believed to be.

Although, realistically but inconsistently with his own principles, Hume sometimes makes covert references to findings that could have resulted only from active investigations, his official view of causation is that of an inert, incorporeal observer. Thus we read in the *Treatise*:

> Tho' the several resembling instances, which give rise to the idea of power, have no influence on each other, and can never produce any new quality *in the object*, which can be the model of that idea, yet the observation of this resemblance produces a new impression in *the mind*, which is its real model. For, after we have *observ'd* the resemblance in a sufficient number of instances, we immediately feel a determination of the mind to pass from one object to

its immediate attendant. ... These instances are in themselves totally distinct from each other, and have no union but in the mind, which *observes* them, ... Necessity, then, is the effect of this *observation* ... ([1739] 1978, I.iii.14, pp. 164–5: the last three sets of italics supplied).

So it is those three Cartesian presuppositions, and especially the third, which commit Hume, whether he likes the consequences or not, to a denial of agency and agent powers. The nearest that he comes to seeking a source for the particular idea of 'the liberty of *indifference*' is when he puts it down, in part at least, to '*religion*, which has been very unnecessarily interested in this question' (ibid., II.iii.2, p. 409). Instead, Hume argues that, because it 'means a negation of necessity and causes' (ibid., p. 407), it must be either a pseudo-concept or a concept without any actual objects.

# 4 The Consequent Scandal of Incompatibilism

In so far as 'the liberty of *indifference*' refers to the power of agents to do other than they do do, Hume was certainly right to insist that it 'means a negation of necessity and causes'. For to assert that power, is manifestly inconsistent with maintaining that the agent is necessitated to act in one sense and no other. At the end of section 6 of his first contribution Vesey quotes twice from Warnock, and comments: 'In short the answer suggested by what Warnock says is that if physical determinism is true then the notion of agent causation does not have anything like the application I have taken it to have' (p. 42).

I will sum up the outcome of my previous section, by using various elucidations and distinctions developed earlier. The discussion in section 3 surely shows, rather than suggests, that the thesis of universal physical determinism could not even be understood by anyone who had not, in their own experience of agency, had reason to know that it is false. For, since actions not merely do not, but cannot have physical causes, we know that that thesis not merely does not, but cannot hold true of human actions. And that we are indeed agents, although the scope of that agency varies from person to person and from time to time, is a truth which we can, and cannot but, confirm every day in our own experience. In this understanding, as Kolakowski put it, 'Our hope . . . the desire for freedom . . . is rooted in the very quality of being human'.

I will attempt to dispose of objections to what to Skinner, Davidson and others will appear a stumbling block only after giving Vesey a chance to put those objections with all the force with which they must be put if truth is to prevail.

# An Alternative Compatibilism

GODFREY VESEY

# 1 Disagreement

Antony Flew and I agree on a lot of things, and when we agree we usually say so. This makes it all the more noticeable when we disagree. We disagree about the assumption 'that all our knowledge must conform to objects' (Kant). To Flew this seems to be either 'an assumption which cannot sensibly be challenged', or one I have failed to explain properly. I tried to explain it – in terms of the case of two colour-vocabularies (our own, in which it is true that two sorts of snow are the same colour, and another, in which it is true that they are not the same colour), and of our assuming that our own colour-vocabulary is right. But Flew interpreted my explanation in terms of different forms of life, of the colour-vocabularies being different, as evidence that the word the other people use is not really a colour word. In short, the intended example of the conformity assumption got me absolutely nowhere with Flew.

Clearly I need to provide a more convincing example of the conformity assumption at work, one which Flew can recognize as such. I will try to do so in section 4 below.

First, however, I must draw attention to one major disagreement that remains unresolved from our opening contributions and to one major agreement that emerges from our second round in the debate. I thought Flew and I were in agreement in approving of what Plato says in the *Timaeus* (46c–48a) about two different kinds of causes: things 'which are endowed with mind and are the workers of things fair and good', on the one hand, and things like fire and water, earth and air, 'which, being moved by others, are compelled to move others', on the other. But whereas I go on to approve of what seems to me to be a similar distinction some present-day philosophers make between 'agent causation' and 'event causation', Flew does not. In his second contribution he says the distinction

'between *causing by* an agent and *causing by* an event . . .
is wrong because there is in truth no difference to be
distinguished between these supposed two sorts of causing'
(p. 122). I cannot agree with him about this: I think
there are important differences – the ones I listed in section
2 of my first contribution. For instance, whereas a causing
event is itself caused, and, if it is caused by another event,
that event, too, is caused, and so on, and so on, agents are
beginners of motion, and are at liberty to move or not. An
acknowledgement of this difference is crucial for my
approach to the issue of liberty and necessity.

I think our disagreement must be the result of some sort
of misunderstanding, but I am not sure what sort. Possibly
Flew misunderstands my expression (*a*) 'Brown (an agent)
caused his arm to rise' as meaning (*b*) 'Something Brown
did caused his arm to rise'. This would certainly account
for our disagreement. There is no difference between the
'caused' in (*b*) and the 'caused' in (*c*) 'The shortening (an
event) of the string attached to Brown's arm caused his
arm to rise'. But, as I see it, the assimilation of (*a*) to (*c*)
entails the denial of basic acts, and hence the denial of
agency.

The major agreement that emerges from our second
engagement concerns the meaning of the expression 'X
causes Y'. Flew and I agree in rejecting Hume's 'constant
conjunction and consequent inference' analysis. And we
agree in using the word 'if' in what we ourselves say about
causation. Now, Hume used the word 'if' in part of one of
his definitions of 'cause' ('we may define a cause to be *an
object, followed by another . . . where, if the first object
had not been, the second never had existed*'), but, as Flew
brings out very well, it is not a definition to which he
(Hume), an an empiricist with a Cartesian understanding
of 'experience', is entitled.

## 2 In Place of the Thought-signifying Assumption

Flew and I give different accounts of the equipment – the assumptions, etc. – Hume brought to his reconciling project. It is obvious why: our accounts are geared to what we, *contra* Hume, think is right. Flew thinks Jonathan Edwards' empiricist, but non-Cartesian, account of how we get the idea of causal necessity is right, and so he stresses the Cartesian presuppositions of Hume's empiricist account. I stress the thought-signifying assumption and the conformity assumption because of what I think is right. I have now to say what this is. In particular, what do I think should be put in place of the thought-signifying assumption? And what do I think should be put in place of the conformity assumption? First, the thought-signifying assumption.

The thought-signifying assumption is the assumption that to talk of the *meaning* of what is said is to talk of a thought, that is, something 'that is within us in such a way that we are immediately aware of it' (Descartes). The assumption has clear implications for a theory of communication. Now, Hume, followed by Hartley and the two Mills, father and son, subscribed to the view that association is to the workings of the mind what gravitation is to the movements of matter. Inevitably, the concept of association was put to use by people who wanted to draw out the implications of the thought-signifying assumption for communication. Communication, they concluded, involves a speaker translating his/her ideas into words, and succeeds if the hearer associates the right ideas – that is, ones corresponding to those of the speaker – with the words he/she hears. The words are needed only because we are not telepathic: one person cannot be directly aware of another person's ideas.

Some such theory of communication was common in the nineteenth century. For example:

In order to communicate the trains of our thoughts to others, as well as to record for our own benefit and use our own past trains in the order in which the ideas composing them actually occurred, it was found absolutely necessary to employ sensible signs or marks. Mind cannot work upon mind directly. One person can only devise and use visible or audible signs, which shall impress themselves on the senses of another person, and, by means of pre-determined associations, call up in his mind ideas in a certain order, and at the same time signify to him that those ideas are passing, or did at some previous time pass, in his (the first person's) mind (Bower, 1881, p. 46).

This nineteenth century theory has survived into the twentieth century (e.g. Katz, 1966, pp. 98, 103; Steiner, 1975, pp. 47, 197–8, 294). Following D. J. O'Connor, who called it 'the translation theory of meaning' (O'Connor, 1952, p. 125), Jonathan Bennett has called it 'the translation view of language' (Bennett, 1971, p. 1) and G. H. R. Parkinson, 'the translation theory of under-standing' (Parkinson, 1977, p. 1). Both Bennett and Parkinson contrast the theory with what is said about meaning in the later works of Ludwig Wittgenstein (1889–1951), especially *The Blue and Brown Books* (Wittgen-stein, 1958, pp. 2–3, referred to by Parkinson, pp. 37–44, referred to by Bennett). Wittgenstein's view of meaning is the view I think should be put in place of the thought-signifying assumption.

Wittgenstein dictated what came to be called 'The Blue Book' to his class in Cambridge in 1933–4. It begins with the question 'What is the meaning of a word?' His answer to this question was memorably summed up by John Wisdom, in 1944, in the injunction 'Don't ask for the meaning, ask for the use':

*At last Wittgenstein gave tongue and the quarry went away to the notes of 'Don't ask for the meaning [analysis], ask for the use', and the transformations of the formal mode –* transformations such as these: 'X in saying that S is P is

asserting a general proposition' means 'X in saying that S is
P is using the sentence "S is P" generally' ... (Wisdom,
1953, p. 117).

This can be adapted to give a Wittgensteinian, anti-
empiricist answer to the question 'What is the meaning of
the word "cause"?':

> At last Wittgenstein gave tongue and the quarry went away
> to the notes of 'Don't ask for the meaning of the word
> "cause" [an idea, derived from an experience], ask for the
> use', and the transformation of the formal mode: 'X in
> saying that S is P (e.g. "Glass is brittle") is asserting a
> causal proposition' means 'X in saying that S is P is using
> the sentence "S is P" to imply a hypothetical ("If glass is
> struck it will break")'.

The trouble is, of course, that the quarry does *not* go
away. Flew would, I think, agree with the above formal
mode description of causal propositions. But yet he holds
Jonathan Edwards' version of empiricism. Why? I would
say: it must be because he assumes that some experience is
needed to justify us in making a particular use of a class of
sentences (e.g., the use of causal sentences to imply
hypotheticals), and he thinks that Edwards has hit on what
that experience is; he assumes that without some such
justification we would have no reason to think that there is
a reality to which the use conforms. In short, it seems to
me that Flew makes the conformity assumption, the
assumption he requires me to explain.

# 3   In Place of the Conformity Assumption

The best-known alternative to the conformity assumption is Kant's 'transcendental idealism'. Kant distinguished between empirical concepts, which we are justified in employing because 'experience is always available for the proof of their objective reality' (Kant, [1787] 1933, A.84, B.116) and a priori concepts, namely 'the concepts of space and time as forms of sensibility, and the categories as concepts of understanding' (ibid., A.86, B.118). He agreed with Hume that we need a proof (a 'deduction') of our right to use concepts, but disagreed with him about the sort of deduction needed for a priori concepts, such as that of causation. Whereas Hume 'assumed that all our knowledge must conform to objects', Kant proposed to 'make a trial whether we may not have more success in the tasks of metaphysics, if we suppose that objects must conform to our knowledge' (ibid., B.xvi). A deduction based on this supposition is what Kant called 'transcendental'. To seek an empiricial deduction of a priori concepts, he said, would be 'labour entirely lost' (A.85, B.118).

I shall not attempt, because of limitations of space, to explain what a transcendental deduction is; but I will say what it is not. It is not a proof that causation is objectively real, that is, that it rules in the realm of things in themselves. It is, at best, a proof that it rules in the realm of things as appearances.

Kant was influential but, in Britain at least, not as influential as Hume. A great many twentieth century British philosophers make the conformity assumption. It lies behind the logical atomism that lies behind the notion that the philosopher's task is that of analysis. Russell's logical atomism is empiricist, in the tradition of Locke, Hume and Mill. Wittgenstein, in the *Tractatus Logico-Philosophicus* (1922) made the conformity assumption.

But he made it, not like Russell in the interests of empiricism, but because he was struck by the thoughts (i) that for a proposition to say something, it must be 'a picture of reality' (were it not a picture then one would not be able to understand a proposition one had not previously encountered), and (ii) that a proposition, being a picture, must have a sense that is definite. What is pictured cannot be indefinite. It is this that generates the demand for the 'simple objects' of the *Tractatus* (Wittgenstein, 1922, 3.23; 1969a, p. 63).

In his later philosophy Wittgenstein rejected the notion that there cannot be sense without definiteness of sense, and, along with it, the picture theory (Wittgenstein, 1953, I, 91–115, esp. 99). He abandoned the realism of the *Tractatus*. Our normal forms of expression do not need to be defended by saying that our ways of speaking describe the facts as they really are (ibid., 402). Such a defence had been thought of as like that of justifying a sentence by pointing to what verifies it, but, so far as that goes, it would be better to say that the rules of language are arbitrary (Wittgenstein, 1967, 331).

Unlike Kant, Wittgenstein does not distinguish between empirical concepts and a priori ones. No concepts have an empirical deduction, not even those of colour. 'Do not believe that you have the concept of colour within you because you look at a coloured object – however you look' (ibid., 332). We do not need justifications for our uses of language. In this respect the rules of language are like rules of games: 'if you follow rules other than those of chess you are *playing another game*; and if you follow grammatical rules other than such-and-such ones, that does not mean you say something wrong, no, you are speaking of something else' (ibid., 320). Take the case of 'I promise to do so-and-so'. Unlike 'I intend to do so-and-so', we use it to commit ourselves, morally, to a certain course of action. Does this use conform to an objective reality? Are we justified in using the expression in this way because we have an experience which assures us that there really are moral commitments? We use 'X-events cause Y-events' to commit ourselves to what would happen if an X-event happened. But how do we know there is necessity in nature? Our uses of language are not responsible to an extra-linguistic reality that has to be accepted as given, and to which they must conform to be 'right' (Rhees, 1982). The only rightness, conformity, agreement or harmony there is between thought and reality is the correspondence between a true thought *in* a language, and a fact (cf. Wittgenstein, 1953, I, 429). The language itself does not conform to anything. 'We have a colour system as we have a number system. Do the systems reside in *our* nature or in the nature of things? How are we to put it? – *Not* in the nature of numbers or colours' (Wittgenstein, 1967, 357). In brief, 'the use of language is in a certain sense autonomous' (ibid., 320).

What I would put in place of the conformity assumption is this view of language, the view at which Wittgenstein arrived when he abandoned the realism of the *Tractatus*.

# 4 The Conformity Assumption and Determinism

In my second contribution to this debate I tried, unsuccessfully so far as Flew was concerned, to explain the conformity assumption in terms of different possible colour languages. I had at the back of my mind Wittgenstein's lengthy discussion of possible colour languages in 'The Brown Book' (1958, pp. 130–41). Wittgenstein used imaginary examples, such as that of 'a use of language (a culture) in which there was a common name for green and red on the one hand and yellow and blue on the other' (ibid., p. 134). The example I gave was intended to be a natural-language equivalent of such imaginary examples.

I shall now try again, but this time with an example taken from philosophy: familiar philosophizing about 'physical objects'. Incidentally I am, here, drawing on thoughts I had, and published (Vesey, 1954), quite some time before I came across related thoughts on the same topic in Wittgenstein's On Certainty (1969b).

Consider the statement: 'There is a table in the next room'. Let us distinguish two possible uses of it, the 'phenomenalist' use and the 'physical object' use, and let us talk, accordingly, of it as a 'phenomenalist statement' or a 'physical object statement'. As a phenomenalist statement it is equivalent in meaning to an infinity of statements about actual and possible experiences. Such experiences are (pace Austin) evidence for the physical object statement, but the physical object statement is not equivalent in meaning to the phenomenalist statement. It is logically possible that the phenomenalist statement should be true and the physical object statement false, and vice versa. (This is sometimes expressed by saying that physical objects are 'mind-independent'.)

Suppose, now, that the question is asked 'What justifies our using the statement in the physical object way?' Not stopping to consider what a very strange question this is, but assuming the answer to be 'The existence of physical objects, i.e. mind-independent entities', some philosophers go straight on to the question 'Do we know such entities exist?', which they answer either negatively (e.g. McTaggart, [1906] 1930, ch. 3; Stace, 1934) or affirmatively (e.g. Moore, 1939).

Whether they answer the question negatively or affirmatively, these philosophers agree in one thing: they treat the statement 'There are physical objects' (the statement that, if true, is supposed to justify the physical object use of statements like 'There is a table in the next room') as if it were a statement about physical objects in the same sense as 'Gorgons and harpies exist' (McTaggart's example of a statement he *does not* know to be true), 'There is a unicorn on the planet Mars' (Stace's example of a statement he *does not* know to be true) and 'Here is a hand' (Moore's example of a statement he *does* know to be true) are statements about physical objects. Now, the sense in which the statements 'Gorgons and harpies exist' etc. are statements about physical objects is this: they are statements *in* the physical object language. These philosophers, therefore, treat the statement 'There are physical objects' as a statement in the language it is supposed to justify. Let us call the view expressed by this statement 'materialism'. Then materialism is a *reductio ad absurdum* of the conformity assumption, and of the whole way of philosophizing that is based on it. If the philosopher's statement 'There are physical objects' is not to be incoherent (a bit like someone trying to pull himself up with his own bootstraps) it must be treated, not as a justification, but as an injunction: 'Please use the physical object language'. This injunction is acceptable if it is not meant to stop us using other languages, but, if it is, then I, for one, am not willing to be blinkered by obeying it. Matter is not all that matters to me.

Consider, now, the statement 'X-events cause Y-events'. Let us distinguish two possible uses of it: the 'regular sequence' use and the 'ordinary causal' use. As a regular sequence statement it is equivalent in meaning to statements about what has been experienced to follow what, such as statements about the experience of day following night. As an ordinary causal statement it is used in the way Flew and I recognize in using the word 'if' in what we say about causation. Suppose, now, that the question is asked 'What justifies our using the statement in the ordinary causal way?' As I understand determinism it is the view expressed by the statement that is given in answer to this question. As such, it is like materialism, the view expressed by the statement that is given in answer to the question 'What justifies our using the physical object language?' If the statement of determinism is not to be incoherent it must be treated as an injunction: 'Please use the ordinary causal language' or 'Please try to explain what happens in ordinary causal language'. (Cf. G. H. von Wright, 1983, p. 62: '*Belief* in determinism may influence our orientation in the world and direct our research. It can function as a constant urge to search for causes. But that determinism is true cannot itself be "causal knowledge".') The injunction is acceptable if it is not meant to stop us using other languages. But if it is, then I, for one, am not willing to be blinkered by obeying it. In particular, I want to be left free to use the language of agent causation, the language in which we hold people, not events, responsible, by their actions, for what happens. Plato said that most men think that 'those things which, being moved by others, are compelled to move others' are 'the prime causes of all things'. He opposed this view, saying that we 'ought to explore causes of intelligent nature', meaning by 'causes of intelligent nature' 'those which are endowed with mind and are the workers of things fair and good'. I am not ashamed to agree with Plato.

# 5   An Alternative Compatibilism

Determinism, whether as an alleged item of causal knowledge, or as an injunction asking us to use only the event causation language, is incompatible with people being held responsible for their actions. On the incompatibility of determinism and agency I think Flew and I agree. We disagree only on our reasons for not being determinists. Flew's reason, in brief, is that 'the thesis of universal physical determinism could not even be understood by anyone who had not, in their own experience of agency, had reason to know that it is false'. Were I an empiricist I would stand up and applaud. But I am not an empiricist, because I do not make the conformity assumption. Our linguistic practices are self-standing. Unlike Flew, I am not even prepared to credit determinism with being a coherent causal proposition, that is, something that could be true or could be false.

The only sort of compatibilism I am prepared to accept is the compatibilism of our sometimes talking of agents as causes and sometimes talking of events as causes. So far as our dealings with other human beings are concerned this means our sometimes treating them as responsible beings with whom we can reason, and sometimes treating them as things to be worked upon, perhaps using the techniques of conditioning. The attitudes are very different, but taking one of them towards someone at one time is compatible with taking the other at some other time. There may even be times when one would find it hard to say which attitude one was taking. I once knew someone who was very contra-suggestible. If I wanted him to agree with me I argued for the opposite viewpoint to the one I held. What attitude was I taking towards him?

In his much-reprinted British Academy lecture 'Freedom and Resentment' (1962), Sir Peter Strawson has put this much better than I can:

What I want to contrast is the attitude (or range of attitudes) of involvement or participation in a human relationship, on the one hand, and what might be called the objective attitude (or range of attitudes) to another human being, on the other. Even in the same situation, I must add, they are not altogether *exclusive* of each other; but they are, profoundly, *opposed* to each other. To adopt the objective attitude to another human being is to see him, perhaps, as an object of social policy; as a subject for what, in a wide range of senses, might be called treatment; as something certainly to be taken account, perhaps precautionary account, of; to be managed or handled or cured or trained; perhaps to be avoided, though *this* gerundive is not peculiar to cases of objectivity of attitude. The objective attitude may be emotionally toned in many ways, but not in all ways: it may include repulsion or fear, it may include pity or even love, though not all kinds of love. But it cannot include the range of reactive feelings and attitudes which belong to involvement or participation with others in inter-personal human relationships; it cannot include resentment, gratitude, forgiveness, anger, or the sort of love which two adults can sometimes be said to feel reciprocally, for each other. If your attitude towards someone is wholly objective, then though you may talk to him, even negotiate with him, you cannot reason with him. You can at most pretend to quarrel, or to reason, with him.

Antony Flew and I have been reasoning with one another, not pretending. What more needs to be said?

# One Word More

ANTONY FLEW

'What more needs to be said?', asks Godfrey Vesey, having concluded his third contribution to this debate by quoting an excellent paragraph from Sir Peter Strawson. Had that been all that Vesey had had to add in his third argument then my answer would have been: 'Precious little'. For the only remaining intervention which I have all along wanted to get in somewhere is a belligerently anti-necessitarian comment on certain things very soundly said by Geoffrey Warnock in the two passages which Vesey quoted at the end of his first contribution (p. 41). Since this is one of those matters of fundamental importance upon which we are, I believe, in substantial agreement, I should still like to make that my own last word. But in philosophy, as opposed to politics, it is if possible desirable that people should be right not only in their conclusions, but also in their reasons. So I shall start with matters on which Vesey is, it seems to me, muddled or mistaken.

# 1 'Agent Causation' and 'Event Causation'

Vesey begins: 'I thought Flew and I were in agreement in approving what Plato says in the *Timaeus* (46c–48a) about two different kinds of causes . . .' (p. 141). Certainly we are agreed both about the distinctions that need to be made and about their importance. My objection was, and is, to the misleading terminology favoured by so many philosophers since the 1960s, 'philosophers who . . . do not acknowledge any debt to Plato' (Vesey, p. 9). I thought that I had made this quite clear, both initially in my first and then in my second contribution (pp. 55–6 and 121–2). But since I have twice failed with Vesey, it is obvious that I am bound to fail with others also. I must therefore try again.

To avoid wanton repetition of my own words I will instead once again quote Vesey. He says that I say that 'the distinction "between *causing by* an agent and *causing by* an event . . . is wrong because there is in truth no difference to be distinguished between these supposed two sorts of causing" . . .' (p. 122). Nor is there; *qua* sorts of causing. For if I press a button then I am causing to occur whatever happen to be the consequences of pressing that button; and I am thereby doing this in the same necessitating, physical sense of the word 'cause' as would be involved were that button to have been pushed not by me as an agent but by some such wholly impersonal and unintending event as either a small meteorite or a monster hailstone just happening to fall upon it. (The only exceptions, albeit vital and rule-proving, are those in which one agent causes another to act – causes in the quite different, non-necessitating, moral understanding of the word 'cause' – by either directing attention to, or by himself or herself producing, what that other chooses to construe as their decisive reason for acting in the sense thus morally and non-necessitatingly determined. Two obvious examples are: giving someone cause to celebrate by telling them some splendid news; and causing someone to do what the Mafia requires by 'making them an offer which they cannot refuse'.)

Certainly there are, as between actions causing events and events (which are not actions) causing events, differences of the last importance. But these refer to the causes of the causing event and of the causing action; not to either the causing by this event and by this action or to the effects thereof. And the crux is that the cause of the event will have been a necessitating, physical cause; whereas that of the action has to have been a non-necessitating, moral cause. It is, therefore, altogether beside the point for Vesey to insist: 'I cannot agree with him about this. I think there are important differences ... For instance, whereas a causing event is itself caused, and, if it is caused by another event, that event too is caused, and so on, ... agents are beginners of motion ...' (p. 142). The reasons Vesey is offering here, though excellent reasons, are not reasons why he cannot, but reasons why he must, agree with me!

Let me make a further and bolder suggestion about those somewhat sheepish 1960s philosophers who followed one another in contrasting agent with event causation. The suggestion is that the reason why generally they failed to go on to distinguish our two senses first of 'cause' and then of 'determinism', and why after that they failed to apply such distinctions to the comparative philosophy of the physical and the moral sciences, was in part their unreadiness to learn from their predecessors, and in part the misdirection of their attention brought about by their unfortunate choice of terminology.

## 2 The 'Conformity Assumption'

I am now quite sure that Vesey and I disagree about this, but much less sure how much this disagreement matters in the present context. For a start, I have to confess that the Kantian project which Vesey commends has always seemed to me, ever since I met it first years ago, quite grotesquely wrongheaded: 'Kant proposed to "make a trial of whether we may not have more success in the tasks of metaphysics, if we suppose that objects must conform to our knowledge" ' (p. 146). My very simple-minded, and yet, I fear, far from humble-minded, objection is that beliefs about objects can correctly be accounted knowledge of those objects only and precisely in so far as those beliefs do in fact conform and correspond to whatever is in truth the case about those objects.

When Vesey moves from Kant to Wittgenstein, the first text he quotes seems to me most strongly to support my interpretation of his Eskimo example (pp. 122–3) rather than his: '. . . if you follow rules other than those of chess you are *playing another game*; and if you follow grammatical rules other than such-and-such ones, that does not mean that you say something wrong, no, you are speaking of something else' (p. 147). Just so: if the Inuit employ different words to describe the look of two sorts of snow which to us southrons seem both unequivocally white, then that is presumably because they are referring to something other than the colour of snow – namely, as Vesey so thoughtfully says, to the difference between the look of 'fresh snow' and that of 'snow that is sufficiently hard-packed to support the weight of a man without snow-shoes' (pp. 104–5). With appropriate alterations the same surely applies to Wittgenstein's own case 'in which there was a common name [*sic*] for green and red on the one hand and yellow and blue on the other' (p. 149)?

In his second contribution Vesey at one point asked us

to consider the questions: 'Are what we call different colours *really* the same or different? In other words, which language is right' (p. 105). I answered: 'But here the briefest of considerings leads me to the perhaps too hasty conclusion that this case constitutes no reason for believing either English or Inuit is either right or wrong' (p. 123). Then I proceeded to treat that case there just as I treated it again in the previous paragraph. It appears that this is now the Vesey-approved response: 'The only rightness, conformity, agreement or harmony there is between thought and reality is the correspondence between a true thought *in* a language, and a fact ... The language itself does not conform to anything' (p. 148).

But now, the first of these last two sentences quoted seems to me to constitute a fairly emphatic expression of precisely that 'conformity assumption' which I had understood that Vesey would have us eschew. So perhaps what we are being called upon to reject is only, and quite undisputatiously, the rash, manifestly false assumption that all descriptive concepts have, and can be known to have, actually existing objects. Certainly this is false: there are, for instance, as McTaggart so rightly insisted, neither gorgons nor harpies. Nevertheless, it is equally certain that we cannot allow Vesey his next conclusion: 'If the philosopher's statement "There are physical objects" is not to be incoherent ... it must be treated, not as a justification, but as an injunction: "Please use the physical object language" ' (p. 150).

Why on earth are we being asked to agree with this? What other and better way is there of justifying the concepts of gorgon, harpy, or whatever else, what indeed could there be, other than to show that there actually are gorgons, or harpies, or you-name-its? And whyever should anyone at all pay the slightest attention to an injunction to employ 'the physical object language' unless there are some physical objects to which it can appropriately be applied? Nor should we so readily admit that there is a 'physical object language', as opposed to physical object terms and physical object expressions. For to speak thus of languages (plural) suggests that we are dealing either with different and alternative ways of saying the same things, or else with complementary and compatible ways of talking about different aspects of the same things.

Fortunately, however, Vesey does not succumb to this temptation. But in speaking of 'our sometimes talking of agents as causes and sometimes talking of events as causes' (p. 152) he is, of course, once again misled by that wretched agent causation/event causation terminology. Nevertheless, all that he really does want to say is, not that all, or any, actions are at once both necessitated and not necessitated, but only that we may sometimes treat people as if this was the case, and sometimes as if it was not. And indeed we may, and do; as Sir Peter Strawson so well and so truly says.

# 3 Incompatibilism and the Falsity of Universal Physical Determinism

So now, at long last, it is time to give my answer to the question which Vesey raised at the end of his first contribution. Mine is not, I think, all that different in substance from his. He wrote, it will be remembered, that 'If Warnock's reasoning is valid then, if I accept physical determinism as a true thesis, it would appear that I ought to renounce what I will, for the moment, call "my belief in agent causation" ' (p. 43). What Warnock is here putting forward is a kind of incompatibilism. In this his reasoning is, I believe, and I have tried to show, correct. But I have also argued boldly, as Vesey has just reminded us, that 'the thesis of universal physical determinism could not even be understood by anyone who had not, in their own experience of agency, had reason to know that it is false' (p. 138). In particular, those pieces of human behaviour – those, as Skinner would have us say, behaviours – those behaviours which are actions are not and could not have been necessitated to occur by sufficient physical causes.

Nor is it only such psychological hardpersons as Skinner who will be inclined to see any such contention as scandalous. I well remember, when I first began to say this sort of thing in print (Flew, 1978), how one of my oldest philosophical friends, who has always known more physics than I can ever hope to learn, was, in his generous and overflowing charity, almost invincibly reluctant to believe that I, whom he had always taken to be absolutely sound on such fundamentals, could really have lapsed so totally from a high state of compatibilist and necessitated grace.

I had, even before this comparatively recent fall, often wondered how people thought that they could know – religious revelation apart – that our universe is subject to an absolutely universal, necessitating, physical determinism. But this particular friend, along with other friends and acquaintances with claims to understand twentieth century physics, had over the years been at pains to persuade me that, at the quantum level, indeterminism reigns; or, if not indeterminism, then at least indeterminacy. Yet if this is true – and I make no claim to any competence to determine whether or not it is – how can these scientific wiseacres be so sure that the most complicated things in the known universe – people, the familiar creatures of flesh and blood which we all are – are subject to a total and inescapable physical determinism?

# One Last Try

GODFREY VESEY

Antony Flew has now said that he has twice failed with me to make it clear what his objection is to saying that agents, as distinct from events, are causes. He says that since he has twice failed with me, he is bound to fail with others also. He says he must therefore try again, and in his third contribution he proceeds to do so.

Since this 'great debate' is fast approaching the point at which it must draw to a close, I will leave it to the reader to judge whether or not Flew succeeds at his third attempt. I, for my part, have twice failed to make it clear to him what 'the conformity assumption' is. Like him, in the space remaining, I must try again.

Kant gives examples of concepts whose claims to objective reality are, he says, challenged from time to time. They are the concepts of fortune and fate (Kant, [1787] 1933, B 116–17). This is of some help in explaining the conformity assumption. One can imagine someone saying 'But is there really such a thing as fortune or fate?' But it would have been of more help if Kant had also given an example of a concept our employment of which is not suspect, and yet for which the question of conforming to reality does not arise.

One such concept is that of a promise. It is a feature of our use of the expression 'I promise to do A' that someone who utters it is morally committed to doing A, and, other things being equal, can properly be rebuked if he/she does not do A. Why do we use the expression in this way? I would say: because we choose to; it is up to us how we use the expression; our use of it does not have to be shown to conform to 'what promises really are' for us to be justified in using it as we do.

It might be supposed that there is nothing objective to correspond to, and justify, our practice with the expression 'I promise' because in saying 'I promise' we are not saying something that is true or false; we are *doing* something, promising. But consider the concept of knowing. Someone who says 'I know' *is* saying something that is true or false. So does the concept of knowing have an objective reality which the concept of promising does not have?

G. E. Moore describes knowing as a process, or event, in the mind. He says that the first question about what sort of thing knowledge is is the question: in what does the event or process consist? It is, he says, 'a question which philosophy shares with psychology' (Moore, 1953, p. 25). In line with this, someone might answer the question 'Why do we use the expression "I know" so that "I know S is P" is false if "S is P" is false?', as follows: 'It is because of the nature of knowledge. Knowing is a mental state which is peculiar in that its existence guarantees the truth of what is said to be known. Someone who says "I know" is reporting, or describing, his mental state. If he has correctly identified his mental state as one of knowing that S is P then he is entitled to expect others to take his word for it that S is P. If there were no such truth-guaranteeing mental states then anyone who said "I know" would not be saying something true or false.'

With this may be contrasted what J. L. Austin and Wittgenstein say. Austin likens saying 'I know' to saying 'I promise'. Saying 'I know S is P' differs from saying 'I believe S is P' in something like the way saying 'I promise to do A' differs from saying 'I intend to do A'. Saying 'I know', Austin says, 'is *not* saying "I have performed a specially striking feat of cognition, superior, in the same scale as believing and being sure, even to being merely quite sure": for there *is* nothing in that scale superior to being quite sure. Just as promising is not something superior, in the same scale as hoping and intending, even to merely fully intending. When I say "I know", I *give others my word*: *I give others my authority for saying* that "S is P" ' (Flew, 1953, p. 144). Similarly, Wittgenstein says: 'Instead of "I know it" one may say in some cases "That's how it is — rely upon it" ' (Wittgenstein, 1969b, 176).

Moore made the conformity assumption. He assumed that for it to be all right for us to use the expression 'I know' as we do the use must conform to some reality. The reality he was led to postulate by making the assumption was that of a truth-guaranteeing mental state. *Not* to make the assumption is to say about 'I know' what one says about 'I promise': it is up to us how we use the expression; our use of it does not have to be shown to conform to 'what knowledge really is' for us to be justified in using it as we do.

Finally, does all this help us to understand how the conformity assumption operates in philosophizing about causation? I think it does. Consider the expression 'X-events cause Y-events'. Instead of this one may in some cases say 'If an X-event occurs it will be followed by a Y-event'. Now, is there a reality to which this use of the expression conforms, and, if there is, what is it?

To those who are disposed to make the conformity assumption the obvious answer to the last part of this question is: it is some sort of necessary connection between the cause and the effect, such that if the cause occurs the effect will follow. We are justified in using causal language as we do if there is this connection, and if we can prove, either from experience or by reasoning, that there is. If there is no such connection then someone who says 'X-events cause Y-events' cannot properly be said to say something true or false.

There is a problem with this answer which there is not with the corresponding answer about knowledge. The mental event of knowing, if there is such an event, is immediately accessible to introspection. But the 'necessary connection between cause and effect' is presumably a physical, not a mental, reality. How can one prove, either from experience or by reasoning, that there is what might be called 'physical necessity'?

This was the question to which Hume was led by making the conformity assumption. We can avoid it if we are prepared to say that it is up to us how we use the expression 'X-events cause Y-events'.

I would go further. It is up to us sometimes *not* to use the event-causation language, and to say, instead, that people are causes. We can choose. It is up to us.

# Open to the Floor

ANTONY FLEW

Godfrey Vesey is certainly right about at least one thing: it is high time and overtime for this Great Debate to be flung open to the floor. But I am glad that he made 'One Last Try', for in this he has, I think, succeeded. My difficulty with 'the conformity assumption' lay mainly in its description as an assumption, suggesting that something at least partially hidden was being detected. But, if someone claims that Oedipus was fated to kill his father and to marry his mother, then he is not tacitly, covertly and perhaps unwittingly assuming that these outcomes could not have been prevented by any human action. On the contrary: that is precisely what, rightly or wrongly, for better or for worse, he is, quite openly and deliberately, asserting outright.

The cases of promising and knowing are, of course, different. For to make a promise or to claim to know is to do something rather than to assert the occurrence of a peculiar kind of mental event; although in doing these two sorts of things one is also asserting that one will do what one is promising to do, and that what one is claiming to know is indeed the truth. But if we report, in the second or third person, that someone else either promised this or knew that, then we are again, and very straightforwardly, asserting that something was the case.

In saying that Jack promised this we are saying that Jack did what, by the conventions of his culture (with which we as reporters may or may not identify), constituted the making of a promise to do this. In saying that Jill knew that — and providing always that there is no hesitation or reservation in the employment here of the word 'know' — we are saying both that that is true, and that Jill was in a position to know it. So I take it that anyone who says such things about Jack and Jill, construing their words as I have been construing them, must in so doing be making what Vesey would call conformity assumptions.

Now that we have at long last succeeded in getting this

sorted out, it would appear that Vesey and I are in fundamental disagreement about causation. Manifestly I am, in his terms, one of those who, in this most important case, makes 'the conformity assumption'. For all along I have been maintaining that causes (physical) do bring about their effects; that we do all have unavoidably abundant experiences both of objective physical necessities and of objective physical impossibilities; and that any assertion about causation (physical) simply is an assertion that certain physically necessary connections obtain. This, it seems, Vesey cannot accept. Curiously he goes on to say: 'If there is no such connection then someone who says "X-events cause Y-events" cannot properly be said to say something true or false'. But, surely, if there are no such connections then anyone who asserts that there are must be saying what is unequivocally and categorically false?

Vesey concludes, finally, 'that people are causes. We can choose. It is up to us.' How right he is. For so long as we are alive and conscious we all of us are, and cannot but be, making choices. And these choices are all choices of what to cause or to try to cause. These causings of ours are, however, of two kinds: causings (physical), which physically necessitate their event effects to occur; and causings (moral), which incline but do not necessitate other agents to choose to act in this sense rather than in that. Yes indeed, 'people are causes. We can choose. It is up to us.' And now it is up to you, the reader.

# Bibliography

Aquinas, St T. [c. 1225–74] (1926) *Summa Theologica*, translated by the Fathers of the English Dominican Province (London: Burns Oates and Washbourne).

Aquinas, St T. [c. 1225–74] (1955) *Summa contra Gentiles*, translated by A. C. Pegis (New York: Doubleday).

Aristotle [384–322 BC] (1941) *The Basic Works of Aristotle*, edited and with an introduction by R. McKeon (New York: Random House).

Augustine, St [354–430] (1964) *The Freedom of the Will*, edited and translated by Anna Benjamin and L. H. Hackstaff (Indianapolis, IN: Bobbs–Merrill).

Ayer, A. J. [1956] 'Freedom and necessity', in G. Watson (ed.) (1982).

Bain, A. (1855) *The Senses and the Intellect* (London: J. W. Parker and Son).

Bennett, J. (1971) *Locke, Berkeley, Hume – Central Themes* (Oxford: Clarendon Press).

Binkley, R., Bronaugh, R. and Marras, A. (eds) (1971) *Agent, Action, and Reason* (Oxford: Blackwell).

Boring, E. G. (1950) *A History of Experimental Psychology* (New York: Appleton–Century–Crofts).

Bower, G. S. (1881) *Hartley and James Mill* (London: Samson Low and Rivington).

Bradley, F. H. (1883) *The Principles of Logic* (London: Kegan Paul, Trench and Co.).

Brown, R. (ed.) (1970) *Between Hume and Mill, An Anthology of British Philosophy, 1749–1843* (New York: Random House).

Brown, T. (1820) *Lectures on the Philosophy of the Human Mind* (Edinburgh: W. and C. Tait).

Carr, E. H. (1961) *What is History?* (London: Macmillan).

Chisholm, R. M. [1964] 'Human freedom and the self', in G. Watson (ed.) (1982).

Coleman, Alice and others (1985) *Utopia on Trial* (London: Shipman).

Collingwood, R. G. (1940) *An Essay on Metaphysics* (Oxford: Clarendon Press).

Danto, A. C. (1963) 'What we can do', *Journal of Philosophy*, 60, pp. 435–45.

Davidson, D. [1968] 'Agency', in R. Binkley, R. Bronaugh and A. Marras (eds) (1971) and D. Davidson (1980).

Davidson, D. (1980) *Essays on Actions and Events* (Oxford: Clarendon Press).

Descartes, R. [1591–1650] (1985) *The Philosophical Writings of Descartes*, translated by J. Cottingham, R. Stoothoff and D. Murdoch (Cambridge: Cambridge University Press).

Edwards, J. [1756] (1957) *Freedom of the Will*, edited by P. Ramsey (New Haven, Conn.: Yale University Press). (The original title was, significantly, *Freedom of Will*.)

Edwards, P. (1967) *The Encyclopedia of Philosophy* (New York: Macmillan; London: Collier–Macmillan).

Einstein, A. (1950) *Out of My Later Years* (London: Thames and Hudson).

Flew, A. G. N. (ed.) (1953) *Logic and Language*, second series (Oxford: Blackwell).

Flew, A. G. N. (ed.) (1964) *Body, Mind and Death* (New York: Collier–Macmillan).

Flew, A. G. N. (1975) *Thinking about Thinking* (London: Collins Fontana).

Flew, A. G. N. (1976) *Sociology, Equality and Education* (London: Macmillan).

Flew, A. G. N. (1978) *A Rational Animal* (Oxford: Clarendon Press).

Flew, A. G. N. (1982) 'Another idea of necessary connection', *Philosophy*, 57, pp. 487–94.

Flew, A. G. N. (1984) *Darwinian Evolution* (London: Granada Paladin).

Flew, A. G. N. (1985) *Thinking about Social Thinking* (Oxford: Blackwell).

Flew, A. G. N. (1986) *Hume: Philosopher of Moral Science* (Oxford: Blackwell).

Flew, A. G. N. (ed.) (1987) *Readings in the Philosophy of Parapsychology* (Buffalo, NY: Prometheus).

Freud, S. [1901] (1960) *The Psychopathology of Everyday Life*, translated by E. Tyson (London: Hogarth).

Galileo, G. [1623] (1957) *The Assayer*, in *Discoveries and Opinions of Galileo*, notes by S. Drake (New York: Double-day).

Galileo, G. [1632] (1953) *Dialogue concerning the two chief world systems – Ptolemaic and Copernican*, translated by S. Drake, foreword by A. Einstein (Berkeley, CA: University of California Press).

Gassendi, P. [1624] (1959) *Exercitationes paradoxicae adversus Aristoteleos*, edited and translated by B. Rochot as *Dissertations en forme des paradoxes contre les aristoteliciens* (Paris: J. Vrin).

Hartley, D. [1749] (1834) *Observations on Man, His Frame, His Duty and His Expectations*, 6th edn (London: Thomas Tegg and Son).

Hobbes, T. [1588–1679] (1839–45) *Works*, edited by William Molesworth (London: Bohn).

Hornsby, J. (1980) *Actions* (London: Routledge and Kegan Paul).

Hume, D. [1739] (1978) *A Treatise of Human Nature*, edited by L. A. Selby-Bigge, revised by P. H. Nidditch, 2nd edn (Oxford: Clarendon Press).

Hume, D. [1740] (1978) *An Abstract of a Treatise of Human Nature*, in D. Hume [1739] (1978).

Hume, D. [1748] (1975) 'An Enquiry concerning Human Understanding', in *Hume's Enquiries*, edited by L. A. Selby-Bigge, with revisions by P. H. Nidditch (Oxford: Clarendon Press).

Hume, D. [1741–77] (1985) *Essays Moral, Political and Literary*, edited by E. F. Miller (Indianapolis, IN: Liberty Classics).

James, W. (1891) *The Principles of Psychology* (London: Macmillan).

Jones, E. (1920) *Papers on Psychoanalysis* (London: Baillière, Tindall and Cox).

Jones, E. (1926) 'Free will and determinism', in his *Essays in Applied Psychoanalysis* (New York: International University Press).

Kant, I. [1787] (1933) *Immanuel Kant's Critique of Pure Reason*, translated by N. K. Smith (London: Macmillan).

Katz, J. J. (1966) *The Philosophy of Language* (New York: Harper and Row).

Kenny, A. (trans. and ed.) (1970) *Descartes: Philosophical Letters* (Oxford: Clarendon Press).

Kenny, A. (1975) *Will, Freedom and Power* (Oxford: Blackwell).

Kolnai, A. [1966] 'Agency and freedom' in G. Vesey (ed.) (1968).

Lehrer, K. (ed.) (1975) *Freedom and Determinism* (Atlantic Highlands, NJ: Humanities Press).

Leibniz, G. W. [1710] (1951) *Theodicy*, edited and translated by A. M. Farrer and E. M. Huggard (London: Routledge and Kegan Paul).

Lessnoff, M. (1976) *The Structure of Social Science* (London: Allen and Unwin).

Locke, J. [1690] (1975) *An Essay concerning Human Understanding*, edited by P. H. Nidditch (Oxford: Clarendon Press).

Long, A. A. (1971) *Problems in Stoicism* (London: Athlone).

Luther, M. [1525] (1969) *The Bondage of the Will*, in E. G. Rupp, A. N. Marlow, P. S. Watson and B. Drewery (eds and trans.) *Luther and Erasmus: Free Will and Salvation* (Philadelphia: Westminster).

McCann, H. (1975) 'Trying, paralysis and volition', *Review of Metaphysics*, 28, pp. 423–42.

McTaggart, J. McT. E. [1906] (1930) *Some Dogmas of Religion* (London: Arnold).

Malebranche, N. [1674–5] (1980) *The Search after Truth*, translated by T. M. Lennon and P. J. Olscamp (Columbus, OH: Ohio State University Press).

Mill, J. [1829] (1869) *Analysis of the Phenomena of the Human Mind*, a new edition with notes illustrative and critical by Alexander Bain, Andrew Findlater and George Grote, edited with additional notes by John Stuart Mill (London: Longmans, Green, Reader and Dyer).

Mill, J. S. [1843] (1974) *A System of Logic Ratiocinative and Inductive*, edited by J. M. Robson, introduction by R. F. McRae, in *Collected Works of John Stuart Mill* (Toronto: University of Toronto Press; London: Routledge and Kegan Paul).

Moore, G. E. [1939] 'Proof of an external world', Annual Philosophical Lecture to the British Academy, reprinted in G. E. Moore (1959) *Philosophical Papers* (London: Allen and Unwin).

Moore, G. E. (1953) *Some Main Problems of Philosophy* (London: Allen and Unwin).

O'Connor, D. J. (1952) *John Locke* (Harmondsworth: Penguin).

O'Shaughnessy, B. (1973) 'Trying (as the mental "pineal

gland")', *Journal of Philosophy*, 70, pp. 365–86.

Owen, R. [1816] (1972) *A New View of Society, or Essays on the Formation of the Human Character*, with introduction by J. Saville (London: Macmillan).

Papineau, D. (1978) *For Science in the Social Sciences* (London: Macmillan).

Parkinson, G. H. R. (1977) 'The translation theory of understanding', in G. Vesey (ed.) *Communication and Understanding*, Royal Institute of Philosophy Lectures, vol. 10, 1975/76 (Sussex: Harvester).

Plato [c. 428–c.348 BC] (1961) *The Collected Dialogues of Plato*, edited by E. Hamilton and H. Cairns (New York: Pantheon).

Pohlenz, M. (1959) *Die Stoa*, 2nd edn (Göttingen: Vandenhoeck and Ruprecht).

Popper, K. R. (1957) *The Poverty of Historicism* (London: Routledge and Kegan Paul).

Pratt, V. (1978) *The Philosophy of the Social Sciences* (London: Methuen).

Priestley, J. (1777) *The Doctrine of Philosophical Necessity Illustrated* (London: J. Johnson).

Rhees, R. (1982) 'Language and reality', *The Gadfly*, 5, pp. 22–33.

Rose, S., Kamin, L. J. and Lewontin, R. C. (1984) *Not in Our Genes* (Harmondsworth: Penguin).

Ryan, A. (1970) *The Philosophy of the Social Sciences* (London: Macmillan).

Schlick, M. [1931] (1939) *Problems of Ethics*, translated by D. Rynin (New York: Prentice-Hall).

Schopenhauer, A. [1841] (1960) *An Essay on the Freedom of the Will*, translated by K. Kolenda (Indianapolis, IN: Bobbs–Merrill).

Sellars, W. (1976) 'Fatalism and determinism', in K. Lehrer (ed.) (1976).

Skinner, B. F. (1948) *Walden Two* (New York: Macmillan).

Skinner, B. F. (1953) *Science and Human Behaviour* (New York: Macmillan).

Skinner, B. F. (1971 and 1972) *Beyond Freedom and Dignity* (New York: Knofp; London: Cape).

Skinner, B. F. (1973) *Beyond Freedom and Dignity* (Harmondsworth: Penguin).

Smith, A. [1776] 'Letter from Adam Smith, LL.D. to William Strahan, Esq.', in D. Hume (1741–77).

Sowell, T. (1980) *Knowledge and Decisions* (New York: Basic).

Stace, W. T. (1934) 'The refutation of realism', *Mind*, 43, pp. 145–55.

Steiner, G. (1975) *After Babel, Aspects of Language and Translation* (Oxford: Oxford University Press).

Strawson, P. F. (1962) 'Freedom and resentment', *Proceedings of the British Academy*, 48, and in P. F. Strawson (ed.) (1968) *Studies in the Philosophy of Thought and Action* (Oxford: Oxford University Press), P. F. Strawson (1974) *Freedom and Resentment* (London: Methuen), and G. Watson (ed.) (1982) *Free Will* (Oxford: Oxford University Press).

Taylor, R. (1966) *Action and Purpose* (Englewood Cliffs, NJ: Prentice–Hall).

Thalberg, I. (1967) 'Do we cause our own actions?' *Analysis*, 27, pp. 196–201.

Tucker, A. [1768] (1834) *The Light of Nature Pursued*, 3rd edn (London: Thomas Tegg and Son).

Valla, L. [1405–57] (1968) 'Dialogue on free will', translated by C. E. Trinkaus, in E. Cassierer, P. O. Kristeller and J. H. Randall (eds) *The Renaissance Philosophy of Man* (Chicago, IL: University of Chicago Press).

van Inwagen, P. (1982) 'The incompatibility of free will and determinism', in G. Watson (ed.) (1982).

Vesey, G. N. A. (1954) 'Unthinking assumptions and their justification', *Mind*, 63, pp. 226–33.

Vesey, G. N. A. (1961) 'Volition', *Philosophy*, 36, pp. 352–65.

Vesey, G. N. A. (ed.) (1964) *Body and Mind* (London: Allen and Unwin).

Vesey, G. N. A. (ed.) (1968) *The Human Agent*, Royal Institute of Philosophy Lectures, vol. 1, 1966/7 (London: Macmillan).

von Wright, G. H. (1983) 'On causal knowledge', in C. Ginet and S. Shoemaker, (eds) *Knowledge and Mind* (Oxford: Oxford University Press).

Warnock, G. J. (1963) 'Actions and events', in D. F. Pears (ed.) *Freedom and the Will* (London: Macmillan).

Watson, G. (ed.) (1982) *Free Will* (Oxford: Oxford University Press).

Watson, J. B. (1913) 'Psychology as the behaviorist views it', *Psychological Review*, 20, pp. 158–77.

Watson, J. B. [1924] (1957) *Behaviorism* (Chicago, Ill.: University of Chicago Press).

Watts, G. [1732] (1811) 'An Essay on the Freedom of Will in God and in Creatures', in *The Works of the Reverend and Learned Isaac Watts D. D.*, edited by D. Jennings and P. Doddridge (London: J. Barfield).

William of Ockham [c. 1285–1349] (1969) *Predestination, God's Foreknowledge, and Future Contingents*, translated by Marilyn M. Adams and N. Kretzmann (New York: Appleton–Century–Crofts).

Wilson, J. Q. (1977) *Thinking about Crime* (New York: Vintage).

Wisdom, J. (1953) *Philosophy and Psycho-analysis* (Oxford: Blackwell).

Wittgenstein, L. (1922) *Tractatus Logico-Philosophicus* (London: Kegan Paul, Trench, Trubner).

Wittgenstein, L. (1953) *Philosophical Investigations*, translated by G. E. M. Anscombe (Oxford: Blackwell).

Wittgenstein, L. (1958) *The Blue and Brown Books* (Oxford: Blackwell).

Wittgenstein, L. (1967) *Zettel*, edited by G. E. M. Anscombe and G. H. von Wright, translated by G. E. M. Anscombe (Oxford: Blackwell).

Wittgenstein, L. (1969a) *Notebooks 1914–16*, edited by G. H. von Wright and G. E. M. Anscombe, translated by G. E. M. Anscombe (Oxford: Blackwell).

Wittgenstein, L. (1969b) *On Certainty*, (Oxford: Blackwell).

Yolton, J. (1966) 'Agent causality', *American Philosophical Quarterly*, 3, pp. 14–26.

# Index of Names

# Index of Notions

This index is intended: not to provide an inventory of all the concepts mentioned or employed in the text above; but to serve as a checklist for student revision. It therefore aims to include only the main ideas, arguments and distinctions needed not just to follow but to participate in fruitful discussion of *Agency and Necessity*.